MONSTER GARAGE

HOW TO

FABRICATE

DAMN NEAR ANYTHING

KEN VOSE

Discovery
CHANNEL

MOTORBOOKS

This edition first published in 2005 by Motorbooks, an imprint of MBI Publishing Company, Galtier Plaza, Suite 200, 380 Jackson Street, St. Paul, MN 55101-3885 USA

Motorbooks titles are also available at discounts in bulk quantity for industrial or sales-promotional use. For details write to Special Sales Manager at MBI Publishing Company, Galtier Plaza, Suite 200, 380 Jackson Street, St. Paul, MN 55101-3885 USA.

ISBN-13: 978-0-7603-2194-2
ISBN-10: 0-7603-2194-9

Printed in China

Discovery Communications book development team:
Jane Root, Executive Vice President, General Manager,
    Discovery Channel
Thom Beers, Executive Producer, Original Productions
Sharon M. Bennett, Senior Vice President,
    Strategic Partnerships & Licensing
David McKillop, Executive Producer, Discovery Channel
Michael Malone, Vice President, Licensing
Carol LeBlanc, Vice President,
    Marketing & Retail Development
Jeannine Gaubert, Art Director, Strategic Partnerships
Erica Jacobs Green, Director of Publishing
Erica Rose, Publishing Associate

MBI Publishing Company book development team:
Acquisitions Editor: Lee Klancher
Associate Editor: Leah Noel
Cover Designer: Rochelle Schultz
Designer: Brenda C. Canales

CONTENTS

fabricate/fabrikayt/v.
construct, manufacture, build, erect, frame, raise, put up, set up, assemble, fashion, figure, form, make, produce. invent, create, originate, devise, formulate, design, hatch, think up.

This book's title, *How To Fabricate Damn Near Anything*, sounds like an invitation to grab some tools and build whatever you want, from a motorized widget to the space shuttle. And well, if you've been watching *Monster Garage* for the past couple of years, you know that Jesse and the gang *really* will attempt to fabricate damn near anything—whether that be an ultimate surfmobile, semi-truck chopper, or swamp buggy.

But what exactly does the word *fabricate* encompass? Construct, manufacture, build, assemble, fashion, figure, form—these processes are all included. So are invent, create, formulate, and design. That pretty much seems to cover the gamut of the dictionary's description of the word.

While we can't promise that after reading the book you'll be able to construct the next Indy 500 winner or a water taxi for trips down to the *Titanic*, we can promise that you'll be better informed about the entire fabrication process. Your *Monster* skill levels and confidence in using them will also be ratcheted up a notch or two.

How To Fabricate Damn Near Anything will explain several basic fabricating techniques so that you can accomplish the task at hand and have all the up-to-date information on using the best equipment to execute your project. In addition, there are insider tips from Discovery Channel's *Monster Garage* pros, who share the knowledge and techniques they've gained in their experience, which you can adapt to your own projects. The fabricators included here may come from diverse backgrounds and may be decades apart in age, but they all have at least one thing in common: They learned their amazing skills by watching others, asking questions, and engaging in trial and error and some good old-fashioned hard work.

Three of the self-taught fabricators featured in this book have taken the "fabricate damn near anything" concept to a level that boggles the mind. Although their stories might be categorized more as "see what you can do" rather than "see how you can do it," they are perfect examples of what can be accomplished when you refuse to believe that it can't be done.

The first, Rick Dobbertin, turned his dream of building an oceangoing amphibious vehicle into reality when he drove/sailed his converted milk tank truck to South America via the Caribbean Island chain. Now if that isn't a monster project, what is? He also is currently in the final stages of construction of his newest amphibious vehicle, the *HydroCar.*

Then, California hot rodder Al Teague gives insight on how he built a racing streamliner in a tiny garage with just some basic hand tools, an air compressor, a drill press, a reciprocating saw, an oxyacetylene welder, and a torch set. He eventually took the completed car to the Bonneville Salt Flats and set a world land speed record, blasting across the salt at more than 400 miles per hour.

Finally, Eddie Paul, who has built everything from movie stunt autos to aircraft to military lasers, describes in fascinating detail the process of building a mechanical great white shark that makes the fish in *Jaws* look like a large rubber bath toy.

In a world that places increasingly more emphasis on technology and higher education, these craftsmen stand apart. They actually get their hands dirty building pretty amazing stuff. And while architects and engineers are heralded for the design of their latest bridge or building, those structures really are only as strong as their weakest weld. In fact, because of the continued construction of everything from large skyscrapers to custom-designed products, those with strong fabrication skills are likely to be in demand in the workforce for years to come. As Los Angeles Trade Technical College welding professor and *Monster Garage* participant Lisa Legohn simply puts it: "A great welder will always have a job."

Another recent development detailed in this book is how designing and machining custom mechanical parts can now be done online, thanks to people like Jim Lewis, who created the software and a website easy enough for a mass audience to use. His company estimates that it reduces the engineering and administrative time for a single custom part from 40 hours to only 15 minutes. "Although not as fast, it's almost like the transporter in *Star Trek*," Lewis says. Read on, and we'll put that notion to the test.

Also profiled are fabricators like Jerry Bowers, who helped craft both a hot rod school bus and racing wheelchair for *Monster Garage*; Mark Carpenter, one of the box truck wrestling ring builders featured in Episode 38; Eric Scarlett, who helped create a Porsche golf collector in Episode 6; and Boyd Coddington, longtime hot rod builder and talent on Discovery Channel's *American Hot Rod*. Then more tips come from Ron Krol, a steel tank designer who worked on the fire truck brewery in Episode 46; Renee Newell, a longtime welder and sculptor; Joe Barnes, a do-it-yourself race car builder; and Ed Federkeil (a custom pickup truck builder) and Todd Blandford (a hydraulics expert), who both helped craft the ultimate tailgating vehicle in Episode 31. Put it all together and what do you have? *How to Fabricate Damn Near Anything*. Now, it's time to get wrenching.

CHAPTER

1

SHOP SETUP & BASIC TOOLS

A well-set-up shop is key to doing good work. You don't need a ton of space, but you will need the right equipment.

"A man can't have enough tools."
— Eddie Paul, Hollywood car builder

When it comes to setup, no fabrication shop is the same. If you plan, as Eddie Paul does, to be able to build a hundred movie cars in a month, as well as craft V-8 motorcycles, mechanical horses, and sharks, you'll need a lot of space—and everything from a Phillips screwdriver to full 3-D AutoCad capability. But if you plan to work on one car (or maybe one bus) at a time, you'll need a shop setup similar to the one *Monster Garage* builder Jerry Bowers works out of.

Yet no matter what you're working on, you'll need a space to actually get the project done. The garage is probably the most typical place for a shop, and if you have an extra-deep garage or a spare bay, you are in luck. If you don't, but have some space on your property, adding a small room onto the back or side of your garage is a possibility. Or if you are handy at all, you can pay someone to pour a slab and frame up the room, and you can do the Sheetrocking and finish work. This is going to be a shop after all—if your finishing skills are subpar, life goes on. You aren't going to be entertaining dinner guests out there!

If you are pouring a fresh slab and have to deal with cooler weather, consider in-floor heating. For a shop, it is ideal. The system circulates fluid through hoses in the concrete, and the warm floor is comfortable to work on. Using this kind of heat can be quite efficient, particularly if you use an electric on-demand water heater.

For those who don't have a garage or space for one, a basement or spare room is another possible location for your shop. The walk-out basement can be a decent place to build your shop, though you have to be wary of generating fumes and noise pollution into the above portion of the house.

The amount of space required for your shop will vary quite a bit, depending on your needs. Simply setting up in a corner of the garage, with a workbench, good light, ample outlets, and clever use of space, can be enough to do simple projects. If you are going to use larger equipment, such as welders, lathes, and sheet metal breaks, you will need more space to work with. Consider one stall of your garage, about 400 square feet, as a great starting place for an advanced shop. Also bear in mind that you will nearly always fill whatever space you create.

Having the right tools is the key to setting up a good shop. They don't need to be the latest, most expensive tools to do the job, either.

The best way to figure out the amount of space you need is to carefully draw up a plan for your shop. Place all the equipment you'll need in it, and be sure to allow ample work space around each tool. This method isn't foolproof, but it will help you figure out how much space is enough.

When setting up a shop, you are going to need plenty of electrical power. In a typical garage, 100-amp service is normally plenty of juice, even if you have a 220-volt outlet or two. If you are using a power-hungry combination of lifts, hoists, in-floor heating, or multiple welders, you may need more power. The key is identifying what kind of equipment you are going to be using, so lay out a map for where each piece goes (there's that layout again); and then calculate your electrical needs.

Another key to setting up a good working shop is to properly light it. You can't do quality work if you can't see what you are doing. Sounds pretty basic, but you'd be surprised how many shops look like something out of the dark ages. Keep in mind that the type of lighting is less important than the quality. In other words, whether it's natural, fluorescent, direct, indirect, or whatever, it needs to clearly illuminate the work areas that are to be used, ideally to the point of eliminating shadows entirely if possible.

Here's an area where auxiliary lighting is a great help and is economical. Portable light banks are available at home improvement stores for less than $50, and they are ideal for working on projects in which overhead light doesn't suffice (when working under the hood of your car, for example).

Expert fabricator Rick Dobbertin says he uses a lot of fluorescent lighting in his shop. "Set the light banks up with three or four switches in a way that you don't always have to have every light on all the time," he says. "This will save on the bulbs and the electricity. Sometimes I'll work all day and never turn anything on except the lights over the workbench."

Placement of outlets is another key point in planning your shop setup. You'll want lots of outlets near the workbench(es) and on the walls in work spaces. Bear in mind that you'll want to be able to use welders and other electrical equipment in any part of the shop.

The physical location of your shop equipment, tools, workbench, storage facilities, and so on should be decided upon before you move everything in rather than after. A good workbench is one of the single most important items in your shop. If space permits, you might even consider having two of them, one made of wood with locking casters so you can move it around the shop and the other of metal, which can be used for welding, hammering, or other heavy work. Also don't forget to bolt a vise securely to one corner of the table.

TOOLS

A toolbox and a complete set of brand-name tools, both metric and standard, is another essential part of setting up your shop. Buying a fairly comprehensive basic set will cost between $200 and $700, and the lower-priced 150-or-so-piece set is a good starting point for beginners. Higher-end tools will cost you quite a bit more. They are a bit nicer to work with, but are a hard expense to justify unless you work with your tools 40 hours a week.

If you have time on your hands, you can find used tools for less. Hand tools can be found everywhere from your local hardware store to flea markets and garage sales. Don't turn your back on some of the bargains to be found in nontraditional outlets.

HydroCar builder Rick Dobbertin has had good luck picking up more expensive tools at swap meets, and he's not afraid to work with unknown brands. "Proper tools don't have to mean expensive tools," he says. "I like having multiple tools of the same thing. I have five air die grinders, each set up with a different tool; a couple of carbide burrs; a bunch of C-clamps (from 2 inch to 10 inch) a sanding disc; a barrel sander; and a polisher. It saves time not having to change the heads every couple of minutes. I bought all five air grinders for under $50 about 10 years ago. They all still work. With proper care, the cheap stuff will work for years."

RECOMMENDED HAND TOOL LIST

The following is a list of the tools every fabricator should have in his or her shop:

1/4-INCH DRIVE SOCKET SET
- 4-millimeter 6-point socket
- 5-millimeter 6-point socket
- 6-millimeter 6-point socket
- 7-millimeter 6-point socket
- 8-millimeter 6-point socket
- 9-millimeter 6-point socket
- 10-millimeter 6-point socket
- 11-millimeter 6-point socket
- 12-millimeter 6-point socket
- 13-millimeter 6-point socket
- 3/16-inch 6-point deep socket
- 7/32-inch 6-point deep socket
- 1/4-inch 6-point deep socket
- 9/32-inch 6-point deep socket
- 5/16-inch 6-point deep socket
- 11/32-inch 6-point deep socket
- 3/8-inch 6-point deep socket
- 7/16-inch 6-point deep socket
- 1/2-inch 6-point deep socket
- 9/16-inch 6-point deep socket
- Quick-release ratchet
- 1 1/2-inch extension bar
- 3-inch extension bar

3/8-INCH DRIVE SOCKET SET
- 9-millimeter 12-point socket
- 10-millimeter 12-point socket
- 11-millimeter 12-point socket
- 12-millimeter 12-point socket
- 13-millimeter 12-point socket
- 14-millimeter 12-point socket
- 15-millimeter 12-point socket
- 16-millimeter 12-point socket
- 17-millimeter 12-point socket
- 18-millimeter 12-point socket
- 19-millimeter 12-point socket
- 9-millimeter 6-point deep socket
- 10-millimeter 6-point deep socket
- 11-millimeter 6-point deep socket
- 12-millimeter 6-point deep socket
- 13-millimeter 6-point deep socket
- 14-millimeter 6-point deep socket
- 15-millimeter 6-point deep socket
- 16-millimeter 6-point deep socket
- 17-millimeter 6-point deep socket
- 18-millimeter 6-point deep socket
- 19-millimeter 6-point deep socket
- 3/8-inch 12-point standard socket
- 7/16-inch 12-point standard socket
- 1/2-inch 12-point standard socket
- 9/16-inch 12-point standard socket
- 5/8-inch 12-point standard socket
- 11/16-inch 12-point standard socket
- 3/4-inch 12-point standard socket
- 13/16-inch 12-point standard socket
- 3/8-inch 6-point deep socket
- 7/16-inch 6-point deep socket
- 1/2-inch 6-point deep socket
- 9/16-inch 6-point deep socket
- 5/8-inch 6-point deep socket
- 11/16-inch 6-point deep socket
- 3/4-inch 6-point deep socket
- 13/16-inch 6-point deep socket
- 7/8-inch 6-point deep socket
- 5/32-inch hex bit socket

In addition to the right tools, you should have plenty of small containers on hand for parts, bolts, and materials. Old plastic food containers and coffee cans are great catchalls.

- 3/16-inch hex bit socket
- 7/32-inch hex bit socket
- 1/4-inch hex bit socket
- 5/16-inch hex bit socket
- 3/8-inch hex bit socket
- 5/8-inch 6-point spark plug socket
- 13/16-inch 6-point spark plug socket
- Quick release ratchet
- 3-inch extension bar
- 6-inch extension bar
- 3/8-inch to 1/4-inch adapter

1/2-INCH DRIVE SOCKET SET
- 12-millimeter 6-point standard socket
- 13-millimeter 6-point standard socket
- 14-millimeter 6-point standard socket
- 15-millimeter 6-point standard socket
- 16-millimeter 6-point standard socket
- 17-millimeter 6-point standard socket
- 18-millimeter 6-point standard socket
- 19-millimeter 6-point standard socket
- 20-millimeter 6-point standard socket
- 21-millimeter 6-point standard socket
- 22-millimeter 6-point standard socket
- 23-millimeter 6-point standard socket
- 24-millimeter 6-point standard socket

- 25-millimeter 6-point standard socket
- 26-millimeter 6-point standard socket
- 27-millimeter 6-point standard socket
- 3/8-inch 6-point standard socket
- 7/16-inch 6-point standard socket
- 1/2-inch 6-point standard socket
- 9/16-inch 6-point standard socket
- 5/8-inch 6-point standard socket
- 1^1/16-inch 6-point standard socket
- 3/4-inch 6-point standard socket
- 13/16-inch 6-point standard socket
- 7/8-inch 6-point standard socket
- 15/16-inch 6-point standard socket
- 1-inch 6-point standard socket
- 1 ^{1}/16-inch 6-point standard socket
- 1 ^{1}/8-inch 6-point standard socket
- 1^1/4-inch 6-point standard socket
- 1/2-inch to 3/8-inch adapter
- Quick release ratchet
- 3-inch extension bar
- 6-inch extension bar

- Fluke multitester
- Safety glasses
- Universal spoke wrench
- Valve stem remover

- Scientific calculator
- Metric thread pitch gauge
- U.S. thread pitch gauge

COMBINATION WRENCHES
- 6-millimeter combination wrench
- 7-millimeter combination wrench
- 8-millimeter combination wrench
- 9-millimeter combination wrench
- 10-millimeter combination wrench
- 11-millimeter combination wrench
- 12-millimeter combination wrench
- 13-millimeter combination wrench
- 14-millimeter combination wrench
- 15-millimeter combination wrench
- 16-millimeter combination wrench
- 17-millimeter combination wrench
- 18-millimeter combination wrench
- 19-millimeter combination wrench
- 1/4-inch combination wrench
- 5/16-inch combination wrench
- 1^1/32-inch combination wrench
- 3/8-inch combination wrench
- 7/16-inch combination wrench
- 1/2-inch combination wrench
- 9/16-inch combination wrench
- 5/8-inch combination wrench
- 1^1/16-inch combination wrench
- 3/4-inch combination wrench
- 13/16-inch combination wrench
- 7/8-inch combination wrench
- 15/16-inch combination wrench
- 11/16-inch combination wrench

ADDITIONAL HAND TOOLS
SCREWDRIVERS
- Phillips screwdriver #0
- Phillips screwdriver #1
- Phillips screwdriver #2
- Phillips screwdriver #3
- 3/16x4-inch screwdriver
- 1/4x6-inch screwdriver
- Posi-drive #1, 2, 3, 4
- Angle driver (for carb adjustment)

PLIERS SETS
- Sidecut
- Channel lock

Specialty tools, like this engine hoist, are great items to find at swap meets, flea markets, and garage sales.

- Hose clamp crimpers

3/8-INCH T-HANDLE

3/8-INCH AIR RATCHET

3/8-INCH DRIVE ALLEN SOCKETS
- Straight and ball sockets (short and long)
- 3/16-inch to 3/8-inch sockets
- Long 5-millimeter socket

CROW'S FOOT SET
- 3/8-inch to 1 1/8-inch

TORX DRIVER BIT SET
- Up to and including #40 and #45

TORQUE ADAPTER SET
- 3/8-inch to 3/4-inch
- 1/2-inch extension sets
- 2-inch to 12-inch straight

HAND IMPACT DRIVER AND BITS

The Sawzall is another versatile shop tool. It will
cut through just about anything with reasonable
speed, and it's relatively easy to handle.

AIR IMPACT WRENCHES
- 3/8-inch and 1/2-inch

TORQUE WRENCHES (CLICK TYPE)
- 3/8-inch to 288-inch pound
- 3/8-inch to 75-inch pound
- 1/2-inch to 288-inch pound

LINE WRENCHES
- 1/4-inch, 5/16-inch, 3/8-inch, 7/8-inch

CRESCENT WRENCHES
- 10-inch and 12-inch

COMPLETE SET OF METAL FILES
- File handles
- Thread files
- Jewelers' files

FEELER GAUGE (FLAT AND WIRE TYPE)

OTHERS
- 6-inch adjustable wrench
- 3/4-inch pliers with wire cutting slot (6)
- 6-inch long-nose pliers
- 7-inch adjustable joint pliers
- 20-piece hex key set
- 3/8x4^1/2-inch center punch
- 5/32x5-inch pin punch
- 3/8x4^1/2-inch prick punch
- 6-piece impact driver set
- 16-ounce ball-peen hammer
- 36-blade master feeler gauge
- Tire gauge
- 13-piece balldriver hex key set
- Dead blow hammer
- 1/2-inch needlenose vise grips pliers (7)
- Wire cutter
- Channel locks
- Convertible retaining ring pliers
- Double-point scriber (2)
- Single-point scriber
- Safety glasses
- Drill bits (numbered, lettered, and
  fractional—all sizes to 1/2-inch)
- Chemicals (contact cleaner, etc.)
- Hacksaw
- Assorted blades
- Tap and die set
- 1/2-inch pneumatic drill
- Bolt cutters
- Automatic center punch
- Pop rivet gun
- Shop towels
- Flashlight
- Heavy vice

ELECTRICAL
- Digital multimeter (10-amp scale, 300-milliamp scale)
- Battery charger
- Timing light
- Charging system and battery
- Load tester
- Jumper leads (24 inches long)
- Three inductive ammeters
  (14 gauge with 30-amp clips)
- Test light

In addition to the standard hand tools, here are some
more tools you should consider adding to your shop

An angle grinder is an extremely useful tool for working metal. The tool is basically a portable grinding wheel, and it can be used to take off welding slag, round edges, and grind away most types of metal.

(thankfully, they come recommended by experts at *Monster Garage*):

- MIG welder
- Drill press
- Chop saw
- Sawzall
- Air compressor
- Oxy torch
- Saber saw
- Plasma cutter
- Hand grinders
- Vice
- Reciprocating hand saw
- Hole saw
- Band saw
- Deburring tool
- Small lathe
- English wheel
- Tubing bender
- Sheet metal break
- Shrinker/stretcher
- Sander
- Air hammer
- Nibbler
- Jack stands
- Clamps in various sizes
- Tap and die set
- Angle finder
- Level
- Framing square
- Straight edge
- Wire brushes
- Markers

This list is far from complete, given the range of available tools and equipment and the many different types of fabrication for which they were designed. Just remember you can always add tools as you need them, or when you decide whether you really need them or not.

SHOP SAFETY

The most important part of setting up your shop, all the *Monster Garage* fabricators agree, is making it a safe place to work. "Don't attempt anything without the proper safety equipment because you never know what's going to happen," says Mark Carpenter, who helped build the box truck wrestling ring in Episode 38. "By proper equipment I mean things like safety glasses, ear protection, leather work gloves, face shields, cutting goggles, welding helmets, welding jackets, cotton-blend clothing, a first aid kit, and a fire extinguisher." Rick Dobbertin seconds Carpenter's advice, adding: "Have at least one fully charged fire extinguisher handy. Something that took years to build could be gone in seconds if a single spark hits the wrong material."

Another aspect of shop safety is making sure your working area is well ventilated and clean, as well as free of flammable and combustible liquids and objects.

CHAPTER
2

PLANNING YOUR PROJECT

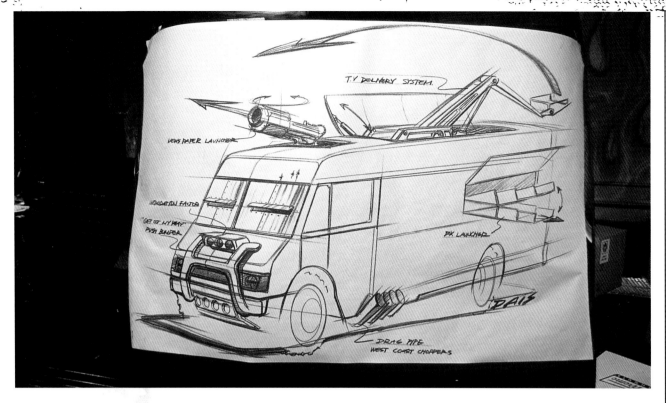

One of the secrets to success on **Monster Garage** is planning the project.

"Plan your build, and build your plan." — Rick Dobbertin, amphibious car builder

While the amount of planning needed to fabricate something like a simple automotive suspension bracket may be miniscule in comparison with that required for the fabrication of an entire suspension system, it does not make the process any less important. In fact, proper planning is the most important step in taking your project from concept to reality. You planned your shop setup based on the types of projects you intended to build there, now it's time to plan the projects themselves.

"One of the biggest mistakes beginning fabricators make is the lack of good planning," race car builder Joe Barnes says. "I've built race cars using a tape measure and a welder, putting things where I thought they should be, or where I'd seen them on other cars. Now I make fully drawn plans so that I know where everything is going to go and what the outcome will be."

The first step is to decide what your project is and set your goals accordingly. Some of the obvious questions you should be asking yourself in this step include the following:

- Do I have the right tools and equipment to do the job?
- How much is it going to cost, and can I afford it?
- How long will it take me?
- Do I have the skill level needed to do the job properly, or will I need help?

Once you start thinking about the project, you'll probably come up with a few more questions to add to that list.

"Then start by laying out your project—draw it, think about it, look at it, check your dimensions to make sure you haven't missed anything," master fabricator Mark Carpenter says. "Take your time. It takes a minute to weld a piece; it will take twice that to cut it out and

Here's an artist's rendering of the planned limo fire truck build featured in Episode 2.

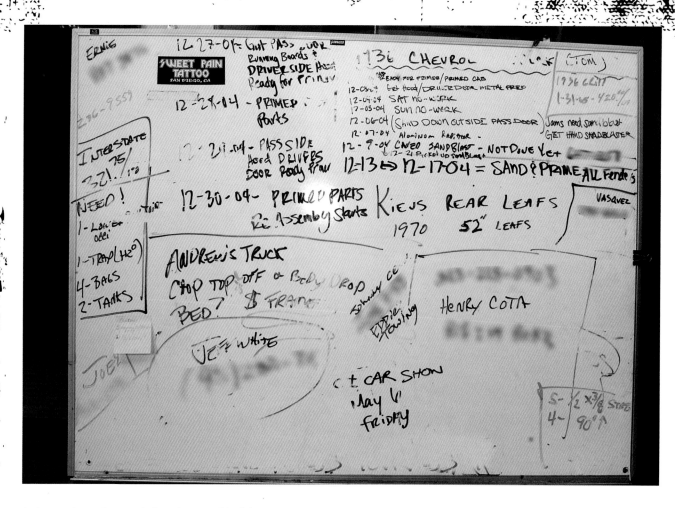

A typical work schedule at a small fabrication shop. The schedule doesn't have to be neat; it just has to do the job.

replace it. That's what you will have to do if it's wrong—or just plain scrap it and start over."

Once you've worked on the project in your mind, now it's time to put those ideas on paper. Your "blueprint" can be as elaborate or rudimentary as you wish; whether it's done on your computer or the back of a paper napkin makes no difference, as long as it is sufficient to get the job done.

Probably the best, and most foolproof, way to layout your project is by making a full-size drawing of the part you want to build. In other words, draw the part so that one inch on paper equals one inch on the finished metal part. This can be done with the simplest drafting tools: a ruler, compass, triangle, and so on, items that can be found anywhere school supplies are sold.

With this layout design, or pattern, you will be able to visualize the completed part—width, depth, height, angles, whatever—before you put tool to metal. Don't rush through this part of the fabrication process. Time spent getting the pattern perfect is time well spent. The pattern itself can be drawn on plain or graph

paper, or it can be drawn onto some sort of poster stock that can easily be used as a template to mark the metal that is to be shaped.

Many fabricators, as you will see, take the completed pattern and use it to make a cardboard mockup of the planned part, allowing them to visualize the part in 3-D without the aid, or expense, of CAD software.

"My approach when starting any project is to visualize, and sort of build it in my head as much as possible," hot rod bus builder Jerry Bowers says. "I go through each process, visualizing and doing accurate drawings. The rule of thumb is always measure twice, cut once. Actually, you can never measure too many times. That's where most people get it wrong, by not thinking it through enough and not measuring enough."

Using your completed "blueprint," make a list of all the materials needed to finish the job: what kind of steel, the necessary hardware, special tools, or other equipment that you may have to buy or borrow. Once you've done that, you'll have a pretty good idea of how long the job will take and how much it is going to cost.

"Most big projects are what I call 'X' jobs," Dobbertin says. "You can estimate the time and the cost, then multiply that by two, or even three times, depending on the complexity, to get an idea of what you're really looking at. If you realize this up front, you won't go as crazy down the road. Planning ahead can save you a lot of time and money."

If you know someone who has done a project similar to the one you're contemplating, talk to them and find out if they encountered any unexpected difficulties, or discovered a shortcut that would work for you as well. If they happen to be more experienced with this type of job, ask if you can call on them for advice if you need it. Instructional books and videos also are great learning tools, but until someone comes up with the technology that will allow them to answer your questions, nothing beats the help of someone who's been there, done that.

"You don't have to go to school to learn how to do this stuff," says Al Teague, who was featured on *Monster Garage* with his lakester build. "Listen to people who know and they'll show you what you need to do. The more you work with it, the more you'll learn."

For certain types of projects, the final stage before you actually put a torch to metal is to make a template of the part out of paper, cardboard, and masking or duct tape. If the diamond that you visualized turns out to be a lump of coal, it's better to find out before you've started the fabrication rather than after.

"I buy 4x8-foot sheets of cardboard and I model everything with it first because it's so much easier to work with than trying to use metal," Dobbertin says.

If genius is, as they say, 90 percent perspiration and 10 percent inspiration, does it follow that fabrication is 90 percent mental and 10 percent metal? Probably not, but you never know for sure.

"On any given job I've only had my welding helmet down maybe 10 percent of the time," says Ron Krol, who helped craft the fire truck brewery tanks used in Episode 16. "The rest of the time is spent planning, measuring, accurately cutting parts, jigging, and pre-assembly."

Percentages aside, the plain truth of the matter is that making a plan is at least as important a part of the fabrication process as is the physical process of cutting, bending, or welding.

FABRICATION: ART OR CRAFT?

The debate concerning just what separates fine art from craft has probably been going on since the days of the cavemen, when perhaps our ancestors who painted the cave walls tried to distance themselves from the guys in the tribe who made designer stone axes. In today's world, the definition is no less clear, as fine-arts sculptors regularly use techniques common to all metal fabricators. Some artists, like John Chamberlin, use parts found in automobile junkyards as the raw material for their works. Even New York's prestigious Museum of Modern Art includes a number of hand-crafted automobiles in its permanent collection.

For sculptors working with metal, the tools and techniques are essentially the same as those used by all of the fabricators included in this book. And for those *Monster Garage* fabricators out there the answer to the art vs. craft debate is simple: fabrication is a craft that can, in the right hands, reach the level of art.

With computer-aided drafting and online part design websites, your PC can help get your project nailed down to a T. **David Pruitt**

RENEE NEWELL

"For me, the love of metal came before welding."

L ooking at the work of artist Renee Newell, the last thing that you'd be likely to think about is welding—a hot, grimy, industrial process that holds just about everything in our modern world together. Yet Renee is a certified industrial welder and a fine art sculptor . . . and admits to being fascinated with fire.

That's part of the reason she got into welding. "At campfires, I'm always the one tending the fire, making sure it's getting air," she says. "So when I first started to weld, it was like, WOW."

As an artist, she has sold numerous pieces, and as a welder, she has done her share of heavy-duty construction work. So she knows both disciplines well.

"There is a big difference between welding a piece of sculpture and doing commercial welding where you are essentially just running a bead," Newell says. "In structural welding, you're going to be putting down bead after bead, and it gets pretty monotonous. Whereas, in sculpture, you are creating. You're not just welding pieces together; you're manipulating the metal."

Newell currently teaches the techniques of welding and metal sculpting to her students at Los Angeles Trade Technical College. This is the same school where she first learned to weld under the tutelage of fellow *Monster Garage* fabricator Lisa Legohn.

"My students aren't coming here to get certified. They want to be able to work the metal for

Renee Newell sees welding as art as much as craft and advises future welders to start with a simple MIG welding box and a good book.

sculpture," Newell says. "I give them the basics, the easy stuff to start with. I start them with an E6013 drag rod, expose them to the MIG machine, and when I think they have the capability, I let them run with it. If any of them did eventually want to get into the realm of public art—large metal sculptures—then they would have to become certified if they wanted to be in charge of the welding and installment."

"For women artists out there who want to work with metal, I'll say that, to me, welding is easier for women," she adds. "I think because there is a certain rhythm involved and a need for patience. But for any artist, regardless of gender, who wants to get into metal sculpture, I'd tell them to get a small MIG machine, because anyone can learn to use it—just get a good instruction book with lots of pictures. Or, if not a MIG, then a little buzz box arc welder, and start with a low amperage drag rod like the E6013; it's easy to control and helps the novice welder to find their rhythm before starting to try and bite into the metal with an E7018."

Newell also suggests using an easy-to-form, easy-to-weld metal, so you won't have to worry about burning holes in the material. Of course, the best thing about metal is that if you do burn through it, you can always fix it. "You you can put back what you've taken off," Newell says.

When done right, welding becomes more than a craft—it becomes an art, Newell adds. "But, as Lisa Legohn is fond of saying, it's not glamorous. Personally, I

Newell uses a plasma cutter to "work the metal" on her newest creation.

don't mind getting dirty, and if you want to weld, neither should you."

Her art dons gallery walls and many pieces have become public art installations.

Working with sheet metal is a key fabrication skill, whether you are repairing an old car body or fabricating fenders for your home-built chopper.

"Metal is easier to cut than most people think. There are a lot of different tools for the job, but no one is right for every type of cut."
— Eddie Paul, Hollywood car builder

Two of the expert sheet metal fabricators who have shared their talents with Discovery Channel's *Monster Garage* really exemplify how different a sheet metal shop can be. Mark Carpenter's MTJ Manufacturing is a large operation, handling machining, fabrication, and assembly of components for commercial and industrial applications, as well as building vertical lifting systems for the material-handling markets. Jerry Bowers, on the other hand, fabricates one-off hot rods and the occasional school bus in his one-man operation.

SPACE

The size of your shop will determine to a great extent the type of work that can be accomplished inside it.

Unless you are constructing a purpose-built building, you will have to make the best use of what you have.

MTJ occupies its own building that encompasses more than 10,000 square feet of space: a 4,700-square-foot shop with a 21-foot ceiling, a 3,200-square-foot shop with a 12- to 14-foot ceiling, and 2,400 square feet of office space. The shop includes a full complement of basic hand and power tools, four MIG welders, a TIG welder, a 400-amp arc welder, a plasma cutter, four band saws, a 65-ton iron worker, a 65-ton mechanical press brake, two lathes, two horizontal mills, two electric and one gas heat-treat ovens, a drill press, a nibbler, full auto-CAD capability, and, as they say in the commercials, "much, much more."

According to Carpenter, a 30x30-foot space is about as small as a practical sheet metal shop can be, although some sheet metal work can be done in a space as small as 16x16 feet, providing there is still room for a decent-sized workbench and a clear area around the work space of at least 3 feet.

Sheet metal fabrication played a significant role in the creation of the ramp that made a Mercedes ML320 handicapped-accessible in Episode 28.

Angle grinders are one of the basic tools of sheet metal work. They can grind off just about any metal and are used for everything from smoothing bodywork to cutting off bolts.

Metal can be shaped and cut using a large grinding wheel.

Chop saws provide a square cut of metal stock, which is particularly useful when building anything that has butt joints.

Sheet metal used to create the firetruck brewery in Episode 46.

The tools and equipment needed by Bowers (listed separately later in this chapter) in his 1,600-square-foot shop obviously are but a fraction of what is available at Carpenter's shop. But, as Bowers puts it, most automotive sheet metal projects can be done in a space the size of a one-and-a-half to two-car garage, except for those pesky school bus builds.

So assuming you have a reasonably large, well-lit and well-ventilated space, what equipment will you need to do the job?

EQUIPMENT

Mark Carpenter recommends the following: basic hand tools, a chop saw, a sawzall, a band saw, a grinder, and a power drill. "For welding, it all depends [on] what you intend to use it for—sheet metal, tubing, small structural, whatever," he says. "Years ago, a gentleman I worked with making filter tanks told me when I was getting ready to expand my shop that I had to make up my mind if I was going to do sheet metal or plate and then buy the appropriate equipment to go that way. I set up for sheet metal and it works fine for everything in 10-gauge or lighter. If I need anything heavier bent, I have to send it out."

Doing any metal fabrication job by hand requires the proper hand tools. In order to "measure twice, cut once," you'll need any of the following: a selection of steel rulers of varying lengths, a retractable tape measure, framing squares, and a combination square set. You'll also want a center punch and a metal compass, or divider, for scribing arcs and circles. After the measuring comes the cutting.

The most commonly used hand-cutting tools are tin snips for making straight line cuts and aviation snips for cutting curved lines. Electric or pneumatic hand shears for cutting heavier steel and a power drill with a hole saw attachment could also be considered essential items.

"It's helpful to have two or three vices, six-inch to eight-inch, at least one with a swivel head," expert fabricator Rick Dobbertin says. "You'll need hammers, chisels, lots of standard and metric box and open-ended wrenches, screwdrivers, pliers, vice grips, and every size and shape of file that you can find."

When it comes to power tools, Mark Carpenter recommends these:

A chop saw: A lightweight (about 30 pounds) portable circular saw. Can be a miter chop saw for wood, with a blade for cutting aluminum.

A sawzall: A reciprocating saw for cutting pipe and plate.

A band saw: Stationary or handheld, it makes more accurate, dedicated cuts than the sawzall.

A disc grinder: Stationary or handheld, it removes bad welds, rust, or paint, and works for deburring rough edges.

A die grinder: Deburs rough edges, grinds down metal to size, and cleans up welds.

A power drill: Makes starter holes for hole saws, installation of hardware, and so on.

Of all the cutting tools available none is more versatile, or makes a cleaner, more professional-looking cut than the plasma cutter. This is the Superman of cutting tools because it is able to cut through a 1/2-inch steel plate as if it were butter and in just about any way you desire. Plasma cutters "cut" by sending pressurized gas through a small channel that holds a negatively charged electrode. When the tip of the cutter touches metal, it creates a circuit that causes a spark that heats the gas, turning it into 30,000 degrees Fahrenheit plasma, which then turns metal molten. Although they are somewhat expensive, plasma cutters are cleaner and easier to use than most other cutting methods.

"The first time I picked one up, I was cutting through steel like it was paper," Eddie Paul says. "I've used them for years; they're fast and easy to use once you get the hang of not quite touching the tip of the cutter to the metal. You have to work with it about a quarter of an inch away."

If you're planning to do larger jobs that hand tools alone can't handle, the most obvious piece of equipment you'll need is a sheet metal break, which is used to bend and cut large sheets of metal. Sheet metal brakes come in a variety of sizes, but the most practical for a small shop is one about eight feet long, as this will handle standard full-sized sheets of metal. Because sheet metal brakes are large and relatively expensive pieces of equipment, it is worthwhile to look for a good used one, preferably a "combination" brake, which will allow you to make multiple bends at angles to each other rather than be restricted to the parallel bends of the standard sheet metal brake.

There are, of course, other large types of sheet metal–forming equipment, including shears and rollers, but they go beyond the scope of what we are discussing here. As we noted earlier, take the time to be sure of what it is that you want to accomplish in the shop and select your equipment accordingly.

MEET THE PROS

MARK CARPENTER

"I love to have people say, 'You made that yourself?'"

Mark Carpenter on the steps of the portable two-piece stairs for a wrestling ring.

Mark Carpenter, president of MTJ Manufacturing Inc. and MTJ Truck Equipment Inc., is a master metal fabricator—a certified welder whose work encompasses everything from custom toolboxes and pool parts to giant truck bodies, fences, shipping containers, wrestling rings, and the odd shrimp boat. His background is typical in that he learned by watching, listening, and practicing, until he got it right.

"Books and videos are a great way to learn, but nothing beats practice," Carpenter says. "You can go to a trade school and take some classes, or try and find someone who can show you what to do. When I was 17, I had a mentor who was a U.S. Navy diver and underwater welder. A mentor is really the way, someone to push you along—try this, try that, looks good, keep it up."

Carpenter's early training came in high school, when he took three years of auto shop. The culmination of his classes came his senior year, when he placed second in the Plymouth Trouble Shooting Contest statewide competition. "A friend of mine had a car that we were putting an engine in and had to weld in a motor mount. When I tried to weld it, some of our classmates started laughing at me, and I said to myself, 'No, that is not going to happen again' and off I went and here I am today," he says.

His fabrication business was a side job for years, something he'd work in after putting in time as a heavy-duty truck and industrial equipment mechanic. "Eventually, I bought a truck body shop from a gentleman who was retiring, and it was tough at first," Carpenter says. "I was a young guy with no real experience running a business like that with a fast-growing amount of overhead. I kept purchasing various pieces of equipment to expand the business. In the late 1980s, I almost lost everything, but I restructured and came back by doing everything right—being straightforward—if it can't be done, be truthful, and don't lie about it."

If there is one aspect of Carpenter's work that makes it stand out from the crowd, it is his custom wrestling rings.

"I got into that through a friend of mine," he says. "The WWE [World Wrestling Entertainment] had bought some scissor lifts that needed to be modified and the supplier could not make the modifications. They wanted to use them sort of like Roman chariots to run the gladiators/wrestlers to and from the ring. So we took the lifts and installed stops to allow a maximum height above the floor of about eight feet to the platform, and we put posts and ropes to make them look like mini-rings. We installed a rear driver's seat with pedals and a steering wheel–operated cable over a hydraulic power steering system like those found on large boats, and then added an electric hydraulic high-volume pump to give it a faster speed. When the wrestlers would get into the platform area, they would raise the platform so as to be able to be seen anywhere from the floor of the arena, and off they went in their chariots."

Now, Carpenter has built between 50 or 55 custom rings, many in different sizes. One was even designed so that it could be dissembled and put into a freight elevator to be moved up to a fourth-floor restaurant. The rings weigh about 4,800 pounds, with the corner posts alone weighing in at about 200 pounds. "We've built so many that we have a jig for every part now," Carpenter says.

The more typical MTJ project, though, is a specialized custom truck body, which can be used in a variety of applications.

The lumber truck MTJ built features a hydraulically operated tilting-slider body with rollers embedded in the bed to facilitate unloading lumber. The body also has multiple tie-down strapping anchors and can be used to lock off different sections of the load to allow multiple deliveries without moving the entire load.

"The truck took about three months [while working on other projects] from start to finish, which included drawing up the all-new design," Carpenter says. "In custom work you have to fabricate just about everything; everything has to be made specifically for that particular truck and checked and double-checked before it leaves here. People don't realize the amount of time it takes to fabricate things. Some items—like hinges, locks, hydraulic cylinders, and valves—can be purchased for less than we can make them in house. As for the other items, it's not

like you can buy them off the shelf—you have to cut everything, fit everything, put it all together, make sure it's square, make sure the customer is getting what they wanted and, most important, what they are paying for. If you don't follow it through with good construction ethics, nothing will be worth a damn. Quality takes time."

The specially designed aluminum striping truck cab was built to replace one that had been damaged beyond repair in a crash.

"We did all the window cutouts first on a bench, then attached the panels to the frame, built the top, sliding rear door, went to paint, soundproofing, then installed it on the truck," Carpenter says.

As for the aforementioned "odd shrimp boat," it is a good example of what a custom fabrication shop can be called upon to build. The boat, a 70-footer, had been partially destroyed in a fire that completely burned off the wheelhouse and crew quarters. The project of assisting in designing and building the crew quarters and wheelhouse was brought to Carpenter after a local shipyard turned down the work for being too small of a project to be bothered with.

"My son and I measured everything, set datum points, made up the drawings, had the drawings approved, ordered the materials, and went to work," Carpenter says. "The wheelhouse is my design. I made up some concept drawings on the computer, laid it out on the floor of the shop with templates, and fabricated it entirely out of aluminum; the same with the crew quarters. They were then shipped to the marina where the pieces where fitted together, welded, and attached to the hull with key lock–type construction, stainless-steel fasteners, and epoxy."

One of Carpenter's less portable works. He never intended to become so well known for his ability to build wrestling rings. World Wrestling Entertainment

3.3
monster project

BUILDING A PORTABLE TOOL CADDY

When we asked Mark Carpenter to think of a project that could be accomplished by someone with a good basic fabrication setup, he came up with something that's not only functional but, as you'll see, eye-catching as well: a portable toolbox/welding caddy.

Although Carpenter based the idea for the toolbox caddy on the ones used by race car mechanics in the pits at the track, this one is intended for use in the shop on a concrete floor. The first step was to decide on the size of the unit. Carpenter wanted to include the toolbox he received for his participation on a *Monster Garage* build, but he also wanted a large, double-size box as well.

When installing the toolbox, make sure to anchor it to the cart by bolting the bottom of the box to the cart frame. When moving the cart, make sure it is on solid level ground, the tanks are secure, regulators are protected, and the drawers are locked.

You might remember Carpenter's earlier comment about the unit being open and not covered in sheet metal. Well, Carpenter being Carpenter, once he looked at the completed unit, he decided it deserved to be diamond plated.

"When someone asks, 'Where did you get it from?' you can say, 'I made it.' And that is what it's all about," Carpenter says. "I feel that way about every piece of equipment that goes out of my shop."

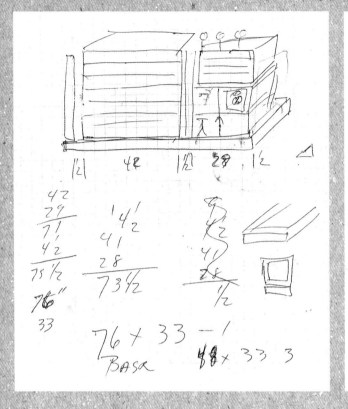

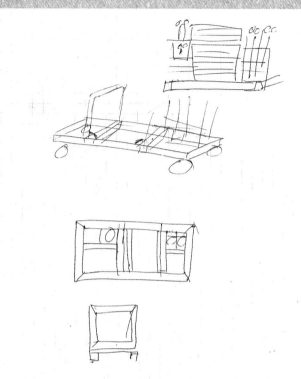

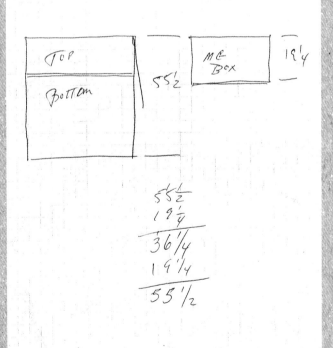

STEP 1 After obtaining the measurements of a larger box, Carpenter made his design sketches for the portable tool caddy. "The unit was obviously going to be heavy, so I knew we'd need large casters since the larger diameter of the wheels would make it easier to roll around," he says. **Mark Carpenter**

STEP 2 The sketches were drawn freehand and at first Carpenter wanted to put the MIG welder and welding gas tank on one end, and oxy and acetylene tanks on the other. But he realized the cart would then be unstable. So in the end, he added a large box with a storage area underneath the *Monster Garage* box, which would house the MIG machine, a welding helmet, a hydraulic jack, and jack stands. **Mark Carpenter**

STEP 3 One of Carpenter's metal workbenches with some of the tools to be used in the build. These include: an electronic welding helmet, safety glasses, welding gloves, cutting goggles, heavy work gloves, a 48-inch T-Square, a 16-inch adjustable square, bar clamps, a hammer and tape measure, framing squares (large & small), a grinder, a drill, a 1/4-inch air/hydraulic riveter, a marker and striker, magnetic clamps, C-clamps, and reference photos. **Mark Carpenter**

STEP 4 To save time on the project, Carpenter used a large-capacity mitering automatic saw to make 45-degree angle cuts on the tube ends for the cart frame. These can be cut with a chop saw, porta-band, or Sawzall, or you can cut the tubes square and deduct for the tube thickness, then buy matching size plastic insert caps to plug up the ends of the tubes. **Mark Carpenter**

STEP 5 When you're laying out the base of the frame, you should always double-check your dimensions and make sure everything is square. **Mark Carpenter**

STEP 6 When squaring up the frame, tack the corners after you have made both sides parallel and the corners square by measuring diagonally. Both diagonal lengths should be the same. Use the bottom frame as a template so you don't have to continually spend extra time setting up each frame. The bottom frame is the jig—from there it's like stacking building blocks. **Mark Carpenter**

STEP 7 Use a small adjustable square to stack the upper frame sections and make sure they are even with the sides of the template frame. **Mark Carpenter**

STEP 8 Here are three frame uprights stacked on the template frame, showing how easily these pieces can be "mass produced." **Mark Carpenter**

STEP 9 Based on the concept drawings of your layout, mark the edge of the frame for the location of the toolbox partitions, just like laying out studs when framing in construction. Carpenter put a line on the lower frame for location of the vertical frame's edge and an X on the side of the line the frame would go on. **Mark Carpenter**

STEP 10 Using the marks for reference, check everything with a tape measure or ruler. When you're dealing with steel tubing, you don't want to have to move it an inch this way and then back again. "Get your reference mark, then double-check it," Carpenter says. "You're not covering this with sheet metal—it's all open, so everything needs to be right on the money." **Mark Carpenter**

STEP 11 If you're doing a project like this by yourself, you'll want to get some clamps or magnetic holding devices to help keep the metal vertical. If using magnetic devices, don't use any that are rated under the weight of the object you are trying to hold in place. And when you're working on something overhead, use a clamp. "They're not cheap; [they] can be as much as $50 or more each, but they sure help," Carpenter says. **Mark Carpenter**

STEP 12 This cast-steel clamp (not cast iron, which is not recommended) is cut in half and welded to the metal workbench. It's used to lock the frame securely in place. **Mark Carpenter**

STEP 13 Laying out the back side of the cart where the three gas tanks will go. Two 1/4x4-inch plates welded flush to the bottom of the lower tubes (one piece with tank separators on top) of the frame will support the tanks. The frame is double reinforced to handle the weight. **Mark Carpenter**

STEP 14 With the magnets holding everything in place, use a small, or adjustable, steel square to make sure everything is positioned equally and square. **Mark Carpenter**

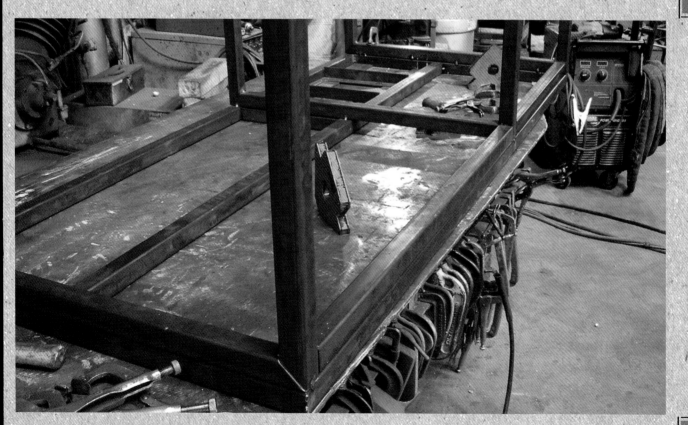

STEP 15 The three upright frames in place. **Mark Carpenter**

STEP 16 The frame, now freestanding and tacked together. A straight edge and long bar clamps keep everything correctly positioned. Before you cut the horizontal tubes that separate the top of the frame, you should always measure from the point where they attach to the base frame. You should measure from the bottom first and cut the tube to match the bottom piece. "Once you get everything all squared at the top, take your bar clamps and get it square in multiple directions," Carpenter says. "I use what I call sacrificial tubing. The tube is tacked into place on the front with small welds, which will help control the warping, on one edge only, so that nothing moves while I'm welding in all of the smaller pieces. When you're finished, just break it off with a wrench by pulling back against the welds." Mark **Carpenter**

STEP 17 After welding metal, you should wait until it is well cooled before you check to see if it is warped. If it is, go back with a torch to correct it. "For example, if you welded two inches, you heat two inches on the opposite side area . . . and heat the metal until it is cherry red," Carpenter says. "Move the torch to keep the metal cherry red for the distance of the weld—it should straighten and will equalize."
Mark Carpenter

STEP 18 With the toolboxes in place, check to see how they fit and how it will look. Mark **Carpenter**

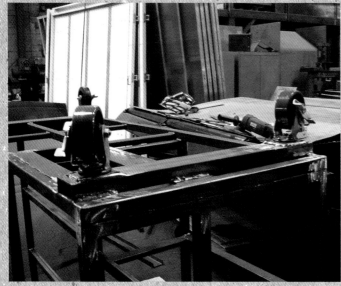

STEP 19 "I like to weld everything, but casters I design to be bolted into place. Six-inch casters will work best," Carpenter says. "There are two swivel casters and two rigid casters, so it can be steered, and all of them have brakes and 200-pound-load capacity each. Don't buy cheap casters. If they collapse and the unit falls over, it'll be a real mess. Always remember, when you roll the unit around you have to lock the toolbox drawers—otherwise, when you go around a corner . . . " **Mark Carpenter**

STEP 20 Circles equal to the diameter of the gas tanks are cut into 3/16th-inch plate, with a 36-inch radius capacity nibbler. A cutting torch, reciprocating saw, or saber saw with a bi-metal blade will also work. They are sheared down the center to create the separating half moons. **Mark Carpenter**

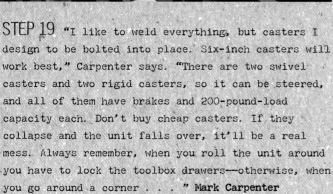

STEP 21 A view of the finished product from the back. **Mark Carpenter**

MEET THE PROS

JERRY BOWERS

"This thing definitely is a square peg, 'cause it sure doesn't fit
into any round holes."

Hot rodders are by nature different from the rest of us when it comes to eyeballing a vehicle. To a hot rodder, every old car or truck is a potential project, something to be chopped, slammed, bagged, tagged, and driven downtown on cruise nights. Yet Jerry Bowers let his hot rodder tendencies go over the edge a bit, if you will, when he decided that his next hot rod would come from a school bus.

Growing up on a small farm in rural Virginia, Bowers first developed his hot rodding interest at an early age, taking things apart and putting them back together again—not always in their original form.

"We were basically poor farm folks and there wasn't much money for store-bought toys and such, so we made our own," Bowers says. "I started by customizing toy cars, and by the time I was in high school I'd moved up to a '37 Chevy coupe. I was about 16, had no equipment, no knowledge, no nothing, but my brothers and I messed around with it a bit."

He took some industrial arts classes in high school, but when he graduated he got a job in a sign shop and worked in that business for 25 years. Yet he always had a car project going on at home—

building a T-bucket roadster with a 318 Plymouth motor, a '53 Merc that was slammed and panel scalloped, a couple of Plymouth ex-cop cars, and a slammed '69 Charger with lake pipes, racing discs, shaved door handles, and frenched lights.

While attending a car show in Maryland in the late 1980s, Bowers first thought about a hot rod project that no one else had yet attempted: building a hot rod school bus.

"I was talking to some other rodders and the subject of school buses came up and why no one had chopped or lowered one, and I thought, yeah, a five-foot-tall school bus—cool," he says.

Jerry Bowers with a work in progress. **Jerry Bowers**

40

"I'd done some work for a guy who had an old 1949 Ford F-5 bus, and we worked out a barter deal for lettering his truck, which is the way it is when you're operating on a shoestring, He towed it over and parked it in front of my shop. It was atrocious."

The bus was built in 27-inch segments, so Bowers and his friends carefully disassembled the sections, then pushed the rear end forward and folded it back together. "Then we started chopping," Bowers says.

His original plan was to fabricate a rectangular tube frame and install a new Ford motor in it, but a friend who owned a salvage yard suggested using the frame of a Cadillac Eldorado instead. It was the perfect solution as the frame was flat, and with front-wheel-drive there would be no driveshaft hump in the floor. When the frame arrived, the body was jacked up, the old frame pulled out, the new one moved into place, and the shortened body lowered onto it. Although it would take some major modifications to make the frame suitable for the heavy bus body, the first major step had been taken. Now the real work could begin, five years of it.

"The top sheet metal wasn't in too bad a shape, but it had coats and coats of paint on it," Bowers explains. "We decided that instead of trying to get it all off, we'd replace most of the sheet metal in the boxed area with .040-gauge aluminum. It ended up with about 80 percent being aluminum, with the front and rear made of steel. The front fenders were widened three inches, raised two inches, and two inches were trimmed off of the bottom of the hood. Everything was MIG welded into a single-section tilt front end. We also designed and built a driver's-side door with an electric window."

Bowers decided, though, that he really wanted to retain the bus' floppy doors and keep them hand operated and at the same proportions they were in the original vehicle. "By the time I was done, it took about eight different cuts to end up with the windows and everything in proportion," he says. "Once it was welded, I sent it off to a friend in Michigan who does bodywork, and he finished them off. My brother Wayne did the upholstery. He took some plywood and foam, carved it out, and it's as plush as can be. We kept the original dashboard, glove box, and instrument panel, and added a Pontiac tilt steering column."

The bus, now christened *Shortcut High*, is almost constantly on tour, visiting schools throughout the country where Jerry and his partner, Brenda, try to impress on students the importance of the bus' motto: Wanna Be Cool, Stay in School. With the program having recently achieved nonprofit status, Bowers is now working on plans to fabricate some new buses in order to get the message out to even more kids.

"I want to give a special thanks to my girlfriend, Brenda, and my brother Dennis," he says. "Without their tireless dedication to the project, *Shortcut High* could never have happened."

Another project near and dear to Jerry's hot-rodder heart is his 1947 Ford four-door sedan–based pickup truck. Built with Ramsey Mosher of Rams Rod Shop (builder of Terry Cook's '39 Lincoln *Scrape*), it was one of the first cars to be turned into a pickup.

"Most people make them out of two-door coupes or convertibles," Bowers says. "I didn't want a two-door body because the doors are too long. To me, they look all out of proportion."

Bowers customized this hot rod pickup, which uses a 1947 Ford four-door sedan front clip mated to a truck rear. He fabricated a Carson-style lift-off top for the hot rod. **Jerry Bowers**

This hot rod school bus, featured on *Monster Garage*, is another Bowers creation. **Jerry Bowers**

EMBOSSED FLAMES

When asked to consider a project for the do-it-yourself rodder with good basic equipment, Jerry Bowers immediately focused on one of the new trends in the rod and tuner world: embossed flames on interior door panels. In fact, he now plans to make similar panels for installation on the pickup.

Depending on the vehicle, flames can be painted or airbrushed onto the panel or, in the case of Bowers' pickup, be left a single color. Leaving them one color more effectively highlights the embossed area.

"A plasma cutter would have worked to cut the flames, but I prefer to use a quality-built reciprocating hand jigsaw," he says. "I've been doing it this way for many years with good results, and it leaves a smooth, even cut line. I also feel I have more control over the project I'm working on. This interior door panel project took me approximately eight hours, and the total cost of material was approximately $150."

Using the right tools for the job at hand is also important. If you're just setting up, Bowers suggests getting what he has in his shop:

- A MIG welder
- Basic air tools
- A large air compressor
- A good reciprocating hand saw

STEP 1 Using chalk, lay out flames on 3-x4-footx3/16-inch flat steel. **Brenda Hoffman**

- A sawzall
- An oxyacetylene torch
- A shrinker/stretcher
- A small metal break

One last piece of advice: "If you're new to this, read as many articles and books as you can find on fabrication; videos are another good source of info," Bowers said.

STEP 2 Using 1/4-inch fine line tape, outline the flames; this gives you a 1/14-inch-wide separation for the top and bottom dies. Then spray silver paint over flames. When it's dry, remove the tape to reveal precise inside and outside cut lines. **Brenda Hoffman**

STEP 3 Drill 3/8-inch holes on each flame tip to facilitate saber saw cuts. **Brenda Hoffman**

STEP 4 The die pieces after 1/4 inch has been removed with the saber saw cuts. Note that the alignment marks are very critical when prepping to compress the dies onto the aluminum panel. **Brenda Hoffman**

STEP 5 Make the first cut inside of the flame design. The saber saw has a reciprocating action that works well on flat steel. **Brenda Hoffman**

STEP 6 Make the second cut on the outside edge of the flame die panel. **Brenda Hoffman**

STEP 7 Bevel the edges of the dies to allow the aluminum to slide when the dies are being compressed. **Brenda Hoffman**

STEP 8 Using the 6,000-pound weight of the bus, the flame design is pressed into the .023-gauge aluminum panel. **Brenda Hoffman**

STEP 9 The panel is now ready to be trimmed and fit into the inside car door panel. **Brenda Hoffman**

RICK DOBBERTIN

"If a little is good ... and a lot is better ... then too much must be just right!"

Like many an expert fabricator, Rick Dobbertin is an old-school, hands-on hot rodder—with a difference. The difference being in just what it is that he's laying his hands on these days: amphibious vehicles. How did a perfectly normal rodder go from building award-winning street machines to sailing a milk tank truck through the Panama Canal? "I had a speed shop where I specialized in superchargers, turbochargers, and nitrous injection," Dobbertin explains. "Then I got to thinking, why not stuff all of these systems into one car?"

"The 1965 Nova SS became my first radical project," he adds. "It was powered by a twin-turbocharged 454 Chevy and was *Hot Rod Magazine*'s Street Machine of the Year in 1982, and the winner of

Rick Dobbertin is a fabricator with a taste for the unusual or outrageous. **Mary Dobbertin**

48

This 1965 Nova was one of Dobbertin's first high-profile creations—a twin-turbocharged big-block-powered car that won accolades from *Hot Rod* and *Car Craft* magazines. **Mary Dobbertin**

Car Craft's 1982 and 1983 Street Machine Nationals. Bringing it to various shows I must have heard a hundred times, 'you've got two turbos, why only one blower?' So, I came up with the idea for the J-2000. I knew it would have to be more than that, so I listed every area that made a pro-streeter a pro-streeter." These included the following:

- A massive engine with a radical induction system
- A racing transmission
- A narrowed rear axle
- Huge rear tires tucked way inside the body
- Narrow front tires, also tucked way in
- A full tubular frame and roll cage
- A very low stance, right on the ground
- Cool graphics and lots of colors
- Safety components, including a five-way harness, fire extinguisher, blower straps, and parachute

"I then decided to shoehorn all of that into the smallest, narrowest car that I could think of to exaggerate it even more," he says. "I ultimately chose the Pontiac J-2000."

When it was completed, the frame was made completely out of polished stainless steel. The engine was an all-aluminum small-block Chevy with aluminum heads. The induction system had two turbos, two superchargers, and nitrous oxide all coupled to a Lenco transmission—the only Lenco ever made out of aluminum instead of magnesium—and graphics by painter Chip Whittington.

Never one to miss an opportunity to go where none have gone before, Dobbertin took the J-2000 to Washington, D.C., for a photo shoot, burned some rubber in front of the Lincoln Memorial and popped the chute.

Rick Dobbertin got into cars because his father worked at General Motors for 34 years. His first wheeled invention was a bicycle that he converted into a hand-pedaled, rear-steer, "monster" when he was 10. He started building cars at age 11 with a Soap Box Derby racer, then progressed to go-karts and hot rods. And it was one of his rods, the J-2000 that, somewhat indirectly, led to his first amphibious vehicle, the *Surface Orbiter*.

"I went to Australia with the J-2000 for six weeks during their bicentennial, and we led the parade through Canberra," he says. "While I was there, I met

Rick's Pontiac J-2000 is outfitted with an aluminum small-block Chevy that breathes nitrous through the only twin-turbocharged, twin-supercharged induction system on the planet. **Mary Dobbertin**

a guy from Sweden and another from Germany who wanted me to bring the car to their countries, and I started thinking how cool it would be to build an amphibious car and drive it around the world."

For most people that would be the end of it—a cool idea perhaps, but that's not Dobbertin. Before long he was looking around trying to find just the right vehicle to modify for his Jules Verne adventure. What he found was a stainless-steel milk tanker. He reasoned that if it could keep 30,000 pounds of milk inside without leaking, it could keep the ocean out. He bought a used tanker for about $5,000, towed it home to his 39x13-foot garage, and started fabricating. Four and a half years and 14,000 man hours later, the tanker had morphed into the *Surface Orbiter*, a 32-foot-long, 8-foot-wide amphibious vehicle the likes of which had never been seen before outside of Hollywood.

Although his plan to circumnavigate the world came up a bit short due to lack of funding, he did manage to cover 30,000 miles on land and 3,000 miles of open water, visiting 38 states and 28 countries. Before the *Orbiter* became the first amphibian to

sail/drive through the Panama Canal, Dobbertin took it across the open ocean to South America, where it received a mixed reception in a number of countries. One local in the Bahamas thought Dobbertin was from outer space.

After all the touring around in the *Orbiter*, Rick dreamed of building another amphibious vehicle, one that would be the world's fastest amphibious craft: the *HydroCar*.

"People were always asking me how fast the *Orbiter* would go in the water. I'd say, 'Ten miles per hour,' and that would be the end of the conversation," Dobbertin says. "So, I decided to build something that would go 50 or 60 miles per hour on the water the *HydroCar*.

"One of the best things about starting from scratch on a project car is you get to design and build every part that goes into it. One of the worst things about starting from scratch on a project car is you have to design and build every part that goes into it."

"I've spent more time on designing and fabricating hinges and latches for the hood, door, and rear hatches than it will take to set up the entire drivetrain. Don't even get me started on the roof drip and

One of Dobbertin's creations at speed in front of the Lincoln Memorial. **Mary Dobbertin**

windshield recess channels. These are parts that make it difficult to get motivated in the mornings."

Like other fabricators, Dobbertin uses cardboard, duct tape, and masking tape to model the parts for proper fit and overall looks before committing to cutting metal. Not surprisingly, the *HydroCar* presented many problems not encountered when building nonamphibious vehicles.

"Amphibians have an entire set of problems that conventional cars are not faced with," he explains. "The number one problem is they have to float—and they need to have their weight distributed in the right places so they don't lean to one side or front to back. They also have an entire set of problems that conventional boats are not faced with. They have to drive down the road, so they can't be too heavy, long, or wide to do that."

Two or three other amphibians have come out that can go 30 or 40 miles per hour on the water since Dobbertin began working on the *HydroCar*, so he

changed his original design from using the 350 engine to the 670-horsepower 572 Chevy. Also, the wheelwells, which were going to be open to the water, will now be completely enclosed inside the sponsons with pneumatically actuated doors like aircraft have, so when the tires go up the entire bottom will be sealed off. The *HydroCar* will be the world's first tunnel-hull hydrofoil amphibian.

"I've done 99 percent of the designing and 100 percent of the welding on the car. I've had people help me form the big sheets of aluminum, which I then trim down and weld. The remaining work—the engine, transmission, axles, and marine drive—all that stuff will be a lot quicker than what's been done so far. Dick Clarke's Colors and Customs will handle the paint. I'll do some road tests with the sponsons off to make sure everything is working properly, then attach the sponsons and put it in the water. It should be done and tested this year and out in public in the spring of 2006."

This wild creation is the *Surface Orbiter*, an amphibious vehicle designed by Dobbertin to be driven around the world. **Rick and Mary Dobbertin**

as wide as possible to permit the tires to steer inside them, as well as to aid in flotation, the body still had to be as narrow as possible. A bulge was built into the middle section to accommodate the driver and passenger.

"The frame took a few months," he says. "It was essential that it be pretty much perfectly square because everything hangs off of the frame; so if it's off by a fourth of an inch here, a fourth of an inch inch there, it'll surely come back to bite you later. The *HydroCar* is within one-sixteenth inch from right to left.

"Another thing that people don't realize is that when you build an amphibian, you can't just drill a hole through the frame for a bolt. You have to weld a tube in the frame, or it's going to fill the frame up with water. You also can't torque those bolts without the tubes because you'll just squeeze the frame together."

Like most hot rodders, Dobbertin is basically a seat-of-the-pants designer and builder. He did make detailed drawings before laying out the *HydroCar* frame, primarily because while the sponsons had to be

The *HydroCar*'s center frame section is stainless steel and all of the sponson parts—frames and skins—are aluminum. Everything was ultimately bonded together with a marine-grade caulk, which, according to Dobbertin, is "a real bear." "I had no way to form the body panels, so I ended up having to cut and TIG weld almost every corner," he says. "It was an arduous task—welded inside and out—I used templates for every-thing. A real time saver was the special chop saw blade for cutting the aluminum that I bought."

Dobbertin used the main stain-less-steel frame as the jig for the sponsons. "It essentially became the welding table for them during the fabrication process," he says. "I foam-filled the sponsons with

Counting all the components and the through-frame tubes (to seal the assembly hardware from the seawater), the *Orbiter*'s frame consisted of more than 900 parts—all welded, ground, and grained to make the frame look like a single piece of stainless steel. Dobbertin has always enjoyed building radical, one-of-a-kind projects. Heck, his initials are RAD. **Rick and Mary Dobbertin**

The *Surface Orbiter* in the Panama Canal. **Rick and Mary Dobbertin**

and use it sparingly. If hanging a door or other body panels, try to keep the gaps to a minimum. Remember, those parts will be around for years to come."

Another thing he says is essential is setting up your workbench well. "Get one sturdier and bigger than you'll ever think that you'll need," Dobbertin says. "You'll need it. I also like having a narrow, movable workbench. This is great for working on two big projects at once, or moving it away from the stationary one to help hold a big section of a project."

When contemplating what he likes best about being a fabricator, Dobbertin says it shares some of the same creative characteristics as writing, painting, or designing buildings. "It takes some sort of compulsive behavior," he adds. "Anybody who spends this much time in the garage can be completely right. People think it's the coolest thing to work on a car all day, but it's just like laying bricks or painting a house—it's labor. I seldom get up in the morning and think, 'Gosh it's seven o'clock, now I get to go out to the garage and work on the car all day.' While it's not always fun, it is rewarding.

"I sometimes look at the people that can afford to just go out and buy a finished car and think to myself, that would be the way to go, but then I stand back and look at something that I created with my own two hands and, I have to say, the feeling that comes over me is something that you just can't buy—although I would like to try it just once."

marine-grade flotation foam, then ground it all down, and painted it with white enamel paint."

"If you don't catch your mistakes someone else will, so you should never move on to the next part of something until the part you're working on is finished," he adds. "If you've got something that's a little bit crooked, don't think, 'I'll straighten it out with the next piece'—well it probably won't happen, and it will compound itself all the way down the line.

"There are a few things that make a big difference in the finished product that only take a few extra minutes and don't cost a dime. I always take the time to round the corners of every bracket I make; it makes them look more finished. I evenly space a series of bolts or rivets, then index the heads [or turn the bolt heads in the same direction] of all the hardware at the time of assembly. Also, always smooth out any caulk,

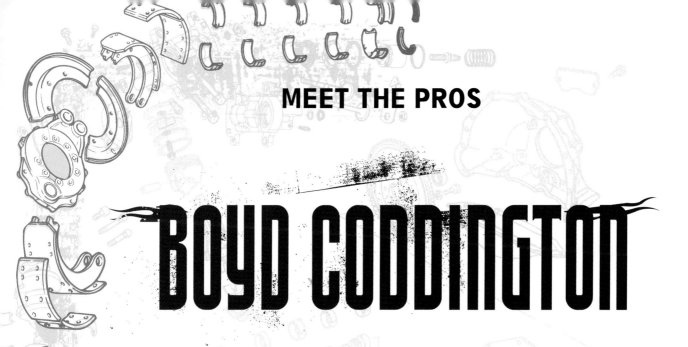

BOYD CODDINGTON

"A hot rod can make you happy."

The name Boyd Coddington has been well known among hot rod aficionados since the early 1980s, when he began making what would become a seemingly endless stream of Oakland Roadster Show favorites. His company, Hot Rods by Boyd, soon became synonymous with artistically designed and superbly executed one-off cars that moved the hot rod from the street to the museum exhibit hall and the cover of *Smithsonian* magazine. Today, his popular Discovery Channel television series *American Hot Rod* has opened the world of rodding to a new generation of fans and future hot rod fabricators.

There are, of course, other hot rod builders, Roy Brizio for example, whose rods are stunning examples of the craft, but with creations like *CadZZilla*, *CheZoom*, the *Aluma Coupe*, and the *Smoothster*, Coddington has proved himself to be a coachbuilder worthy of comparison with the giants of an earlier era, such as Jacques Saoutchik, Henri Chapron, Howard "Dutch" Darrin, and Figoni et Falaschi.

Born in Idaho in 1944, Boyd built his first rod in 1957. A trade school graduate, he worked in a number of local body shops until age 20, when he moved to Salt Lake City to become an apprentice machinist. Apprenticeship completed, he moved to California, married, got a job at Disneyland, and began work on a Model T coupe. The coupe, completed in 1976, was described in *Street Rodder*

magazine as, "a true masterpiece of the street rodder's art." Henry Ford might have had a premonition about this when he predicted that design "will give us a whole new art." For Boyd Coddington, that Model T was the first of what would become more than 300 Hot Rods by Boyd.

One of the most recent examples of the coachbuilder's art as imagined by Boyd is the aptly named *Whatthehaye*. The car's flowing sensuous aluminum body was massaged into shape by Belgian sheet metal master Marcel Delay; its one-off wheels are cut from six-inch-thick aluminum billets. The underpinnings are a modern contrast to the retro design. Power is supplied by an 8.3-liter, 500-horsepower, 10-cylinder Viper engine mated to a six-speed transmission. Clearly an homage to the great French firm of Figoni et Falaschi, which was known for its extravagantly bodied Delahayes, Coddington's *Whatthehaye* is a contemporary example of what the Museum of Modern Art dubbed "rolling sculpture."

In a recent Discovery Channel *American Hot Rod* special, Coddington picked the *Whatthehaye* as his top hot rod, saying this about it: "When you look at it, it grabs you; but when you start it up, it throws you over the edge."

Boyd and his wife, Jo, were both on hand at the 34th annual Barrett-Jackson auto auction in

Boyd Coddington, with his incredible *Whatthehaye*, is a hot rod building legend.

Scottsdale, Arizona, when the *Whatthehaye* went on the block for a staggering $540,000.

After that, Coddington was understandably upbeat about the future of hot rodding. "Hot rodding has become a lifestyle, and a family lifestyle," he says. "In the beginning, it was such an outlaw thing—street racing and jalopies and all that stuff. Now you can take your five- or six-year-old kids to a hot rod show and do things as a family. I think it's great."

And if any more proof is needed to justify the claim that fabrication can transcend the bounds of craft and move into the realm of art, you really don't need to look any further than the elegant creations that have come to be known simply as, Hot Rods by Boyd.

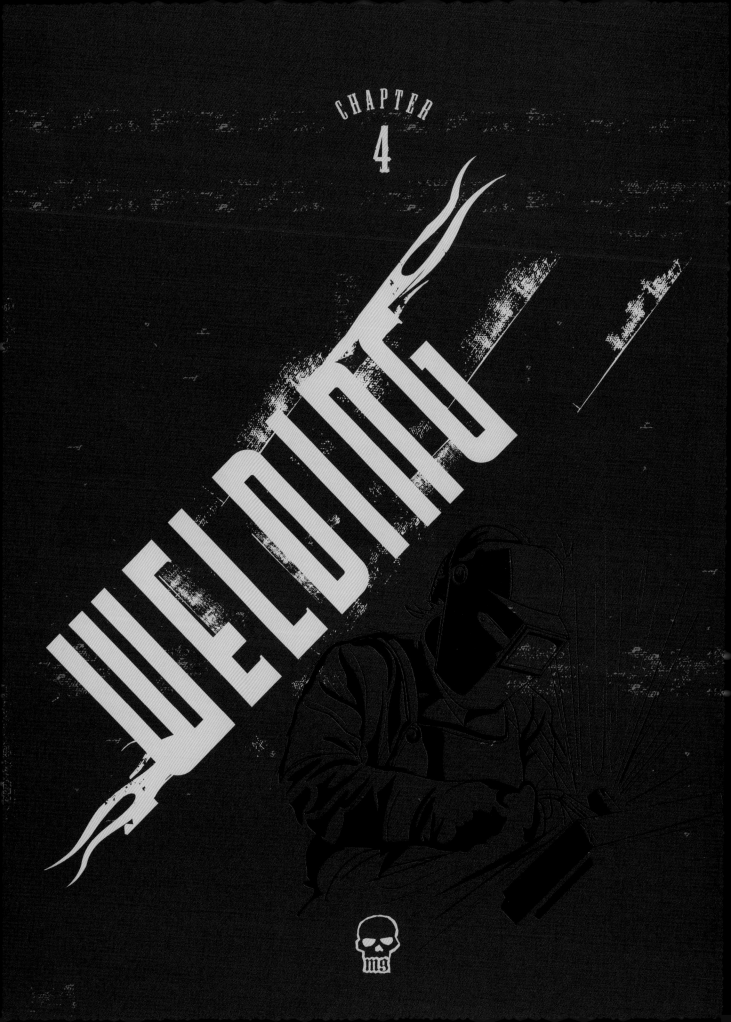

Welding is one of the essential skills to crafting your own personal monster.

"Welding technique is essential."
— Rick Dobbertin, aquatic car builder

Some welding techniques have been around for more than 80 years and are still being used in today's top welding shops, but those early methods—oxyacetylene gas welding and heliarc welding—have now largely been supplanted by two newer processes: metal inert gas (MIG) welding and tungsten inert gas (TIG) welding. In fact, every one of the fabricators included in this book recommended the MIG welder as an essential item for anyone setting up a metal fabrication shop.

"If you're just starting out, I'd recommend a 110 machine, a MIG, or wire-fed machine, which is the easiest process to learn," *Monster Garage* welder Lisa Legohn says. "It's fast—you can learn to do a competent weld in about a week. Get yourself a good basic instruction book like *How to Weld Damn Near Anything*, and practice, practice, practice."

SPACE

A good welding environment requires proper lighting, good ventilation without excessive drafts or extreme cold, and a sturdy metal workbench set at the height most comfortable for working.

EQUIPMENT

As noted, the MIG welder is the first choice for a new shop setup, but as there are a number of different types of MIG units, it will be up to you to choose the one that best fits your purposes.

MIG welders come in different rated amperages, generally between 60 and 160 amps. The higher the amperage, the thicker the metal you can weld. A 100-amp or better unit is good for welding up to 1/4-inch steel.

The MIG works by continuously feeding a thin wire into the weld puddle via an electric motor-drive system, along with an argon gas shield to keep the metal from oxidizing. To operate it, you need only turn on the power, turn on the gas, point the trigger, and weld.

You can also get a "gasless" MIG unit fitted with a flux core wire, which produces the same effect as argon gas, but without the gas bottle. This unit is more portable than the standard MIG.

Depending on the skill of the operator, a MIG

Welding the support system for the buckets on the second Grim Reaper, built on Episode 30.

Safety gloves are a must when welding or using a cutting torch or plasma cutter.

The plasma cutter is the jack-of-all trades of metal working.

machine can weld up to 24 inches of .050 steel per minute, which is nearly four times as fast as the other modern unit, the TIG welder.

"Probably the biggest mistake made when using a MIG is to pull the gun while welding instead of pushing it," Eddie Paul says, "which keeps the gas in front of the weld and produces a much better result."

A TIG welder produces a very high-temperature, very confined arc that heats metal to the melting point for the purpose of fusion welding, yet uses less heat than either MIG or gas welding units. It offers the welder the most control of any welding process and accomplishes fusion without the addition of filler rod, eliminating extra weld seam buildup. Once the arc is struck and a molten weld puddle started, it can be maintained with the unit's amp controls for as long as needed. This means that there is always enough time

Below: A good helmet is another important accessory when welding. Modern models have light-sensing shields that darken when you strike the arc.

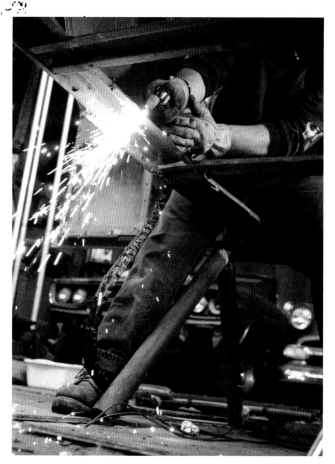

The shop space needed for welding is fairly minimal, and 110-volt wire-feed welders can be purchased for about $200.

to properly add filler rod material to the puddle.

"The TIG makes a nice, even weld, but you have to watch the metals melting," Mark Carpenter says. "You have to know when to fuse it. When you do aluminum, you have to look for the puddle and watch it flow together; a lot of people when they're first starting put the wire in, lay it down, and are done with it. You have to lay the wire in place and melt it to see what's going on. You have to see the joint; if you can't, there's no sense welding the job. If you put too small an amount of heat to it, you won't weld anything, and if you over throttle the control pedal, you'll go right through the material.

"The only way to learn how to do it right is to practice, practice, practice. It doesn't come for free—it takes time. Some people complain that the TIG is hard to work with; well, anything's hard to work with if you don't know how to use it."

Over the years, the oldest welding process, oxyacetylene welding, has remained based upon oxygen and acetylene gas mixing, igniting, and producing a high-temperature flame. This type of unit is primarily used today for cutting torches, but they are still reliable for welding jobs that don't require pinpoint application, as the area heated by the torch is much broader than with either MIG or TIG units.

The welder you select will probably be the single most important initial acquisition for your new shop. Although a name-brand welder may cost a few dollars

Welding stainless steel can be done with MIG (metal inert gas) or TIG (tungsten inert gas) equipment. TIG is very expensive for home use, but provides the ultimate in control.

Welding and cutting face shields are available in battery- and solar-powered versions. If you are intending to only do one type of welding, a fixed shade is fine. If you plan to use a variety of types of welding, a variable shade shield will allow you to adapt it to your task.

more, most fabricators agree these pieces of equipment are worth it. They are generally better built by manufacturers who stand behind their products with warranties and readily available parts in most areas or via the internet. But buying a name-brand welder does not mean you have to purchase new equipment. Tent sales are often a great place to find bargains on name-brand equipment. The internet is also a viable option, the major drawback being that you can't actually see the unit before you purchase it, which can cause obvious headaches.

The most important, and necessary, accessory to your new welding rig is a welding helmet. This is not an item to try and save a few dollars on. The latest technology may cost more, but no one wants to put a price on his or her eyesight. Eye burns from the UV rays present in arc welding can cause cataracts or even eye cancer. The newest welding helmets feature an electronic face shield lens that changes density almost instantaneously as soon as an arc is struck, becoming

three or four times darker. In addition to reducing eye strain, they also contribute to much more accurate arc starts than the older style helmets, which required the torch to be aimed at the weld joint with the helmet shield up, then started once the shield was lowered.

Welding is hot, grimy, and, without the proper precautions, dangerous. And according to Eric Scarlett, who helped build *Monster Garage*'s Porsche golf collector, "You're going to get burned."

In order to melt metal for fusion you need a lot of heat, at least 2,700 degrees Fahrenheit for welding steel. But you can take certain preventive actions to lessen the number of times you singe yourself. These include wearing leather sleeves and gloves and doing whatever it takes to remind yourself not to touch a just-welded joint with your bare skin. You should also always cover all exposed skin when welding as the UV rays can also cause melanoma, or skin cancer, and you must also make sure that anyone else in close proximity to the welding process is aware of its potential dangers.

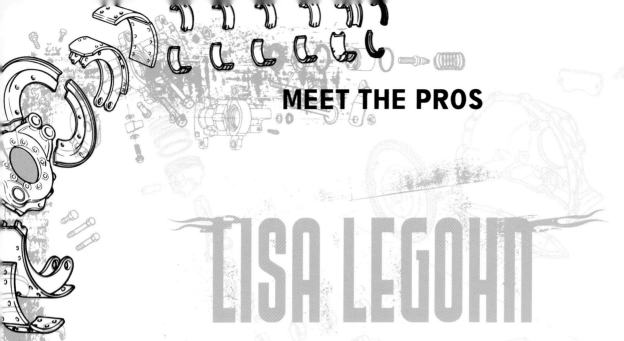

LISA LEGOHN

"My weld is my signature."

Lisa Legohn became a welder because she thought it sounded like a cool—or rather hot—thing to do. As a seventeen-year-old student at Hollywood High, she heard about a welding vocational program through a school counselor, who told her the process was like "fire and a helmet." "I quickly told her to send me there," Legohn says.

Needless to say, she stuck with the program, graduated, and found a career in welding. In 1983 she started teaching welding part time at Compton Community College, and she ended up staying there for 20 years. She is currently associate professor of welding technology at her old alma mater, the Los Angeles Trade Technical College. There she teaches advanced students, the majority of whom will become certified welders, as well as others who need additional training to upgrade their welding skills.

Legohn has appeared on two *Monster Garage* episodes and was a regular on Discovery Channel's *BIG*. She is known in the trade as one who is at the top of her game. So for anyone who wants to buy some welding equipment and learn the basics of the craft well enough to be comfortable doing various fabrication and repair jobs, Legohn is always willing to offer her expert advice.

"People tend to look at welding as just metal hitting metal and sticking together, and it's so much more than that," she says. "It is truly the art of fusion, taking two separate entities and making them become one."

"For most beginners the hardest thing to learn is patience. They'll probably use a lot of mild carbon steel, which melts anywhere from 2,300 to 2,500 degrees," she adds. "It doesn't melt instantaneously. It's not like a microwave oven. You have to allow the metal to melt. Have patience."

She's also quick to point out to those interested in making welding their full-time job that it is not an easy profession. "It's hot, you're going to sweat, you're at close range to 2,300-degree heat, you'll get burned. Believe me, it's not glamorous, and you're not going to get good at it overnight," she says. "There is no instant gratification; it takes a lot of practice."

She recommends that those looking for a career change first look to purchase a good home welding unit and get some practice. An average medium-end 110 home welding unit costs about $450 to $750. "Low-end units have a shorter duty cycle," she says, "which means you have to turn off the unit for a proscribed amount of time after so many hours or minutes of use before you can use it again. Generally, the cheaper the machine, the shorter the time it can be used continuously."

Legohn also likes to remind beginning welders that it takes almost the same amount of effort to make a

Welder extraordinaire Lisa Legohn has been on several *Monster Garage* episodes. She is a welding instructor who loves her work.

junky weld as it does to make a quality weld, so it's always better to spend a little more effort making your welds perfect. "Think about all the bridges in the world, and all of the welds holding them together. A bridge to me is only as strong as its weakest weld," she says.

Other safety tips she often shares include the following: put your helmet on before striking an arc if you have an electric welding machine and remember that all types of welding involve extreme heat and things don't instantly cool down.

ERIC SCARLETT

"All these people say they're fabricators, they can do this or that—well, I can cook hambugers, but I'm no chef."

First Class Autowerks is considered by many, including multiple award–winning designer/builder Doug Deberti, the place to go for custom air bag installations. The shop is also well known for innovative fiberglass work and custom restorations.

Like many of our other featured fabricators, Eric Scarlett, founder and owner of the company, began working on cars at an early age. His grandfather Joe Taormina came to America from Italy and, by the time Scarlett was born, owned a gas station in Tarzana, California, a place Scarlett remembers well.

"Whenever we went to visit their house, I'd go into his garage and watch him work," Scarlett says. "I'd play with his tools, and it really got me into tinkering with toys and then with cars. He put my aunt and both of my uncles through college by working as a mechanic and that made an impression on me, that you could make money doing this."

As a young teenager, Scarlett took some woodworking and metal shop classes with a great teacher, which further sparked his interest in becoming a fabricator. "All of these things together put me into the

mode of 'let's build it, let's do cars,'" he says. "After I learned the basics, I started hanging around with friends who had low-riders—hoppers with hydros. I actually lowered my first truck, a 1973 Datsun, when I was about 14."

Since that time, Scarlett has worked on everything from Ferraris and Lamborghinis to mini-trucks, vans, and at least one 1955 Olds Rocket 88 in his 17 years as a professional fabricator.

"I got started in fabrication by working at other shops to get the experience and soak up their knowledge," Scarlett says. "The guy who really taught me the most was Brian Jendro."

We asked Scarlett to give us some hands-on tips in three areas: welding, fiberglass, and air bags. He was about to replace a damaged section of a rear window channel from a 1936 Chevy pickup undergoing restoration at the shop, so we stayed around and took some pointers. This type of welding job is quite common, not just with automotive repair, but in many different areas.

Eric Scarlett at his shop. He was one of the *Monster Garage* fabricators who helped turn a 1984 Porsche 944 into a golf ball collector in Episode 6.

REPAIRING A REAR WINDOW CHANNEL

Welding is a great way to perform simple repairs. In this project, Eric Scarlett shows how to fix a rear window channel. When prepping 4130 steel, a thin film of rust is acceptable, but it needs to be free of paint, oil, and other contaminants. Clean the steel off with a liquid metal prep that contains phosphoric acid, available at auto body shops.

"One of the great things about welding is that if I mess it up, I can drag it back down and then put it back right. I can cut something in half, make it too short, cut it off again, and extend it a bit," Scarlett says. "Welding is not easy, but it can be fun when you do it right."

STEP 1 First grind the window channel in preparation for removal of the damaged section.

STEP 2 Then lay the channel window panel on a workbench and clamp it to 1x2-inch tubing to keep it flat.

STEP 3 The next step is to cut out the damaged section with a zap saw.

STEP 4 Here's what the window channel looks like after removing the damaged section.

STEP 5 After removing the damaged section, align the channel and smooth the rough edges with a sander.

STEP 6 Then hammer it straight.

STEP 7 Before going any further, remember to compare the old and new channels.

STEP 8 Then mark the cut lines.

STEP 9 Next check the cut lines for the splice.

STEP 10 When done cutting, see how the new section fits.

STEP 11 Using magnetic holders, secure the new section in place.

STEP 12 Then weld in the new section.

STEP 13 Next, clean up the repaired area with a grinder.

STEP 14 Eyeball the overall fit of the window channel.

STEP 15 Next, fit and tack in the new section and make your final welds.

STEP 16 Final welds.

STEP 17 With one more pass from the grinder, smooth out the body line.

STEP 18 Here is the new section, completely welded in place.

MEET THE PROS

ED FEDERKEIL

"Welding is an art."

Ed Federkeil, a fire captain has managed to combine his 23-year firefighting career with two more interesting vocations: drag racing and custom truck fabrication. From the mid-1980s to mid-1990s, Federkeil was a regular on the NHRA tour, winning enough races to land a sponsored ride and some product endorsements. It was during his years of building and driving door slammers that Federkeil also began to do custom truck fabrication.

"The truck thing sort of happened by accident," Federkeil says. "A kid from California, who was one of the crew guys on Darryl Gwynn's top fuel team, was renting a room from me. He bought a half-ton pickup and started ordering mail order stuff for it—a lowering kit, custom wheels—all stuff that really wasn't that common on the East Coast back then. He kept telling me, 'Hey dude, why don't you start building trucks, man?' I thought he was crazy. I'm a drag racer; I don't fool with that stuff. Nobody would pay anything for that. Well, he built his truck in my race shop—and it was pretty cool—so he'd be driving it around and people would ask where they could get one, and he'd send them to me. I was turning them away, but after about 20 guys showed up—when the 21st came in—I said, 'Give me your keys. We're a truck shop.' It took me awhile, but I finally figured out there was a real market there."

Ed Federkeil has done a lot of different kind of fabrication projects over the years—everything from building a drag racing car to crafting a custom pickup truck. In his *Monster Garage* appearance, he helped make an SUV into the ultimate tailgaiting machine.

Today Ed's company builds concept and feature vehicles for both Ford and General Motors for the annual Specialty Equipment Marketing Association (SEMA) show in Las Vegas.

"We build custom trucks; everything from luxury SUV conversions for athletes, celebrities, movie stars, to full air bag setups, to just about whatever anyone wants. I do stay away from things that I believe would not be safe, or from something that would diminish the value of the vehicle. There are guys in this field who are butchers. When I'm done, it's got to be functional, something I'd drive myself," he says.

Federkeil was always heavily involved in sports at school—baseball, wrestling, and football—but he was also into cars. His father had been a stock car racer and, in one of those nice coincidences that sometimes happen, the father of the kid who lived next door to Federkeil's grandmother had built Federkeil's father's race cars.

"When I was 12, I started hanging around with him and also with the guy who lived across the street who had a '65 Corvette," he says. "He started a project on a 1948 Chevy pickup. We'd go to the junkyard for parts, and I'd help out with the work on the car. I bought my first car when I was 15."

Federkeil soon got the drag racing bug, and in his twenties he built a car for bracket racing, which he then uprated to run in the NHRA super gas class. He finally hung up his helmet in order to concentrate on his growing business. He no longer has any doubts that he is indeed a truck builder.

For anyone contemplating this sort of work, Federkeil has a few suggestions about getting started. "If you're going to work out of your garage, you need to have an air compressor, as a lot of your tools are going to run off of electricity or air," Federkeil says. "Also get a MIG welder. Welding is an art. Everybody can probably do it, but there's a select few that can do it as well as Jesse James. And remember, measure twice, cut once. I can't tell you how much stuff I've screwed up because I didn't double-check my measurements before I cut something. If you're on a limited budget, you don't want to be going back to buy another sheet of aluminum, or whatever. And save your scraps, because there's always things that can be made from scraps."

He also said that those looking to do some fabricating in their home shops should have the following equipment: lifts, a drill press, a tubing bender, a sheet metal brake, various standard hand and power tools, and a plasma cutter.

"I know it's a cliché that you can do anything you want to if you want it bad enough, but it's true. It all depends how hard you want to work," he adds.

CHAPTER

5

FIBERGLASS

"Fiberglass is always fun." — Eric Scarlett, Episode 6 fabricator

Fiberglass, or fiber-reinforced plastic (FRP), has been used in thousands of products, not least of which is the Chevy Corvette, which has been clothed in a fiberglass body since its inception. While less durable than steel, it is lightweight and can be molded into almost any shape imaginable. In fact, if damaged, it can be easily patched and used with comparative ease. So for the home fabricator, it probably finds more use in automotive, motorcycle, and marine repair applications than any other function.

To use fiberglass resin, which is available in hardware stores, you must mix it with a catalyst in order for it to set up and harden. Once the proper-sized fiberglass mat or cloth has been cut, you apply a coat of resin with a brush, affix the mat, then cover it with another coat of resin. The number of coats you'll need depends on the nature of the job at hand. Fiberglass is also easily molded by soaking the mat in resin/catalyst, placing it into a shaped mold, and letting it harden. There are a number of different resin/catalyst combinations on the market, each requiring a slightly different procedure for correct application, so an important rule in working with these materials is to carefully follow the manufacturer's instructions.

While there are no specific additional shop space requirements for using fiberglass, you need to ensure that you have adequate ventilation, as the materials involved can have harmful long-term health ramifications.

The chemical components that make up the materials used when laying up fiberglass can cause everything from eye irritation to kidney disease to cancer. So you should always wear proper clothing, including gloves, to minimize contact with exposed skin because some chemicals can be absorbed through the skin. Also never work with fiberglass without wearing a respirator or a mask and some form of eye protection, preferably safety goggles.

Fiberglass can be formed into any shape, and is a fairly versatile material to work with. The drawbacks are it is relatively heavy and requires applying several layers of material, which takes time. The race car street sweeper was a Petty Enterprises car that was converted for Episode 12.

"You can ruin your vision for life in less than a second," Rick Dobbertin says. "We seldom get second chances on this."

In addition to all of the above, keep in mind that many of these materials are highly flammable. So you should store your solvents and resins in their original containers and in a cool, well-ventilated place, as far from heat and sparks as possible.

Race car bodywork is often fiberglass or carbon fibre. Carbon fibre is laid using similar processes to laying fiberglass. The difference is the material, as carbon fibre is much lighter and stronger than fiberglass. This 1999 champ car became a line painter in Episode 32.

BUILDING A FIBERGLASS STEREO ENCLOSURE

In addition to their other automotive fabrication projects, Eric Scarlett and his new partner, Jereme Elwell, do a lot of fiberglass work—not just the usual patching and other typical body repair work, but custom work in a variety of areas.

"I learned how to work with fiberglass by watching other people," Scarlett says. "The first thing I do if I have a big custom job is call in an expert. That's because fiberglass resins hurt my hands. Remember, when you work with fiberglass, you want to use a respirator and gloves."

In this fiberglass project, Scarlett and a colleague are placing a stereo system into the trunk of a 1955 Olds Rocket 88, which is being customized. It already has a full air bag setup, so now it needs some sounds. "We'll have two 12-inch L7 speakers in the corners, an amp, and equalizer on the floor, with a flush cover blending it all together into a single unit," Scarlett says.

"I usually make an outer flush cover, something that will give you the right sort of look when you're done.

"With this kind of fiberglass enclosure, you've got to have a certain amount of air space, or the fiberglass will break from the bass moving the air inside the enclosure. For the speaker box enclosure we use MDF, medium-density fiberboard, not plywood," he adds.

For this project, you'll need some sheets of 4x8-foot fiberglass sheets, which are thin and can be bent almost in half. Other materials you'll need include a gallon of fiberglass resin, some tubes of resin hardener, fiberglass cloth (not matting—because the area you're working with is large), a lot of cheap paintbrushes, and plastic cups to dip them in. "All stuff that can be thrown away when you're done," Scarlett says. "You'll also need a quart of acetone. Usually I tell people to buy a gallon, or even five gallons because it's so much cheaper. You can pick up all the stuff you need at a

STEP 1 This project begins by measuring and cutting pieces of medium-density fiberboard (MDF) to create a frame to hold stereo equipment and several air tanks inside the trunk.

STEP 2 This square rack will hold the amp.

STEPS 3-4 The next step is to measure and cut the MDF to fit around the air tanks.

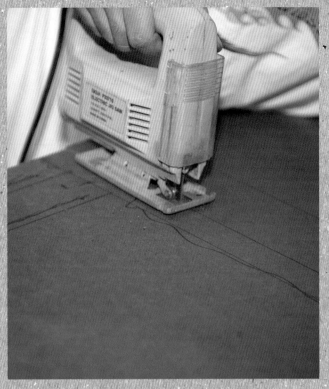

STEP 5 Next, cut the masonite to fit around the front of the trunk opening.

STEP 6 Always check your fit before you go on to making the next cut.

STEP 7 Gather the materials needed for the project.

home improvement store or any number of places. Don't get the cheapest stuff. Go for name brands."

Here's the complete list of materials you need to fabricate the fiberglass stereo enclosure:

- 1 4x8 sheet of medium-density fiberboard (MDF)
- 2 4x8x1/8 sheets fiberglass bend board
- 1 gallon glass filler
- 1 gallon fiberglass resin and hardener
- 4 packages fiberglass cloths
- 1 gallon acetone
- 1 package cheap plastic drinking cups
- 4 yards of speaker fleece
- 1 bag cheap 2-inch paintbrushes
- 1 quart fiberglass primer and hardener
- Dual-action stick back sandpaper and long flat board sandpaper in 36, 80-, and 120-grit gauges
- Miscellaneous fiberglass spreaders
- Miscellaneous 1.5-inch drywall screws

In order to make your final product look as good as an expert's, Scarlett offers this piece of advice: "Like a lot of people, I used to use chicken wire or foam to shape what I was going to do and then laid plastic over it—trash can plastic, or whatever—and then put all the fiberglass over it. What my guy uses is speaker fleecing, the stuff that covers speaker gratings. You can buy it in upholstery shops. It cuts easily with a razor blade."

In this approach, you stretch the fleecing over the fiberboard and fiberglass enclosure, then staple it in place to angled corners. Then you start dipping your resins and putting the actual matting onto the fleecing.

"Once it hardens up, you start building your material—how high you want it, how thick. Then you start sanding it and take out any imperfections," Scarlett says. "We start sanding with a 36-gauge and get progressively finer until it's totally smooth. Then it's just a matter of building it up and sanding it down until you're satisfied that it's smooth enough. I like it to be as smooth as a mirror. Then, at the end, we prime and paint it to match the car. It's a process that takes some time, but it's worth it."

Now the installed components are in place, including two five-gallon air tanks, two 2500 class amps, two capacitors, one 300-amp fuse and fuse holder, and wiring. The enclosure is in primer. When the car is painted, the enclosure will be painted and detailed to match.

For anyone setting up their own small fabrication shop, Scarlett recommends the following:

- A complete set of quality hand tools, metric and standard
- A torch set
- A name-brand MIG welder
- A top-quality 6-horsepower, 60-gallon air compressor
- Miscellaneous hand grinders and sanders
- Jack stands
- A vise
- A good strong workbench

Scarlett also has some final words of advice for those contemplating their own fiberglass project: "If you're just getting into fiberglass, I'd suggest you start by patching something small in order to get used to working with the materials."

STEP 8 Test-fit components as you go, making sure your cuts are accurate.

STEP 9 The rack is now ready to be prepped before being fiberglassed. Scuff the material with 36-grit sandpaper so resin and fiberglass will adhere.

STEP 10 Apply fiberglass fleece to the corners. The fiberglass will adhere to the surface, giving it the desired shape. Above, you see the fleece being stapled tightly in place.

STEP 11 Then mix the resin with the hardener tube.

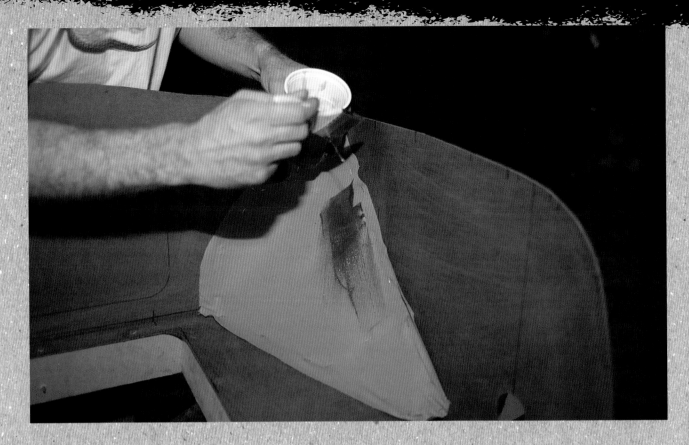

STEP 12 Next apply thick layers of resin for strength. It must be brushed thoroughly so that it soaks through the mat. Also soak it into the wood/masonite for adhesion.

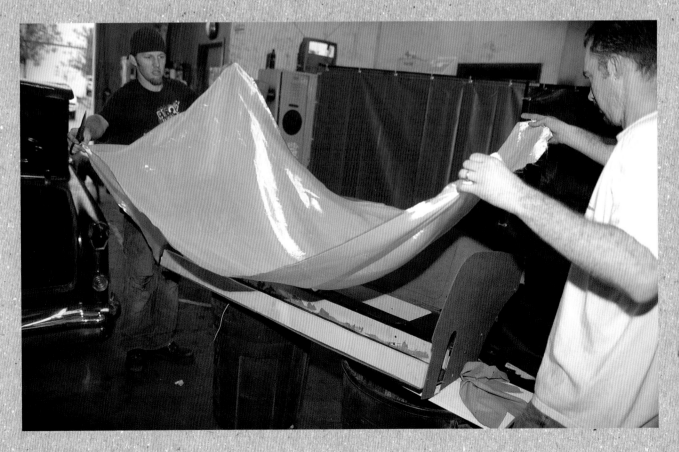

STEP 13 Lay the dry fiberglass mat over the wet resin, and work the mat into the resin.

STEP 14 Work the resin through the mat with a Bondo scraper to avoid lumps.

STEP 15 Then apply more resin. Note that about halfway through the drying process, you should take a razor and trim the rough edges away. If you wait until it's fully dry, it will require a saw.

STEPS 16-17 Next add mat and resin to the back side. Note that you'll want to double-coat corners for strength, and sand everything smooth with a power sander before applying the fiberglass reinforced autobody filler.

STEP 18 Mix the fiberglass reinforced autobody filler with hardener on a flat surface, as shown above.

STEP 19 Spread the filler on the enclosure surface to make it smooth and build it up.

STEP 20 Then file the reinforced auto body filler to get a semi-smooth finish. This will also remove air pockets, which can be filled with another coat of glass.

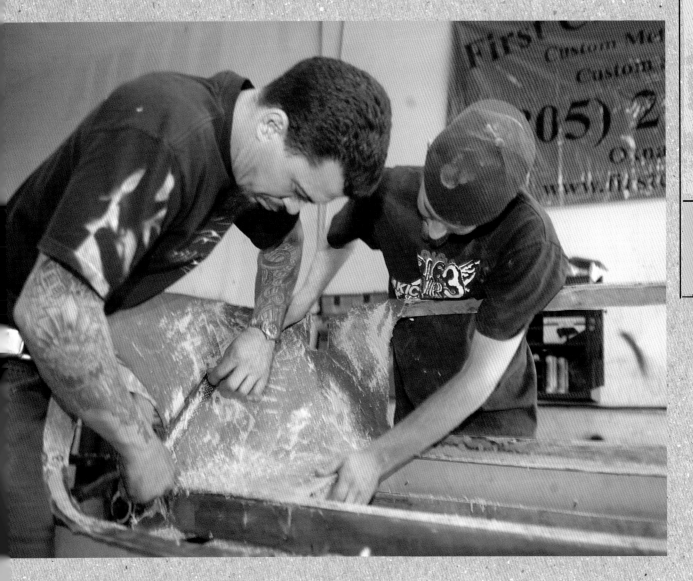

STEP 21 After filling (or cheese grating) the glass, add another coat. Keep up this process until the surface is smooth.

STEP 22 If you need to shape the glass to a curve, sand it with a socket.

STEP 23 Sand with a hand grinder until you have a perfect surface. Final touchup sanding can be done with sandpaper.

STEP 24 Here you see the enclosure unit ready for installation.

STEP 25 Here is the finished product with the air tanks, subwoofers, and amps installed.

CHAPTER
6

MACHINING

"Don't try to over-engineer
everything—reinventing the
wheel. Make it simple and chances
are you'll make it work."
— Al Teague, hot rod builder

While the ability to machine parts will give you more capability to do certain types of jobs, it is not essential for most small fabrication shops, any more than a sheet metal break would be needed by someone who only makes parts for his HO-Gauge model railroad. But if you really want to get into machining, the most common piece of equipment you'll add to your shop is a lathe.

The historical importance of the lathe, which makes accurate machining of cylindrical parts possible, cannot be underestimated. Today's lathes may bear but scant resemblance to those original units, but the principles of operation are essentially unchanged.

A lathe for a small fabrication shop should be a compact, but versatile unit. These are often referred to as "hobby lathes" due to their ability to turn out small precision parts for things like scratch-built models. Before you buy a lathe, consider carefully what you intend to use it for. Just as it's easier to paint a soap box derby racer than a top race car, it's easier, and more economical, to do small machining jobs on a small lathe.

If your workload and budget make sense to do so, adding a vertical milling machine for machining flat surfaces, precision drilling, hollowing out, and other operations not associated with the lathe will give you the kind of versatility not usually found outside of a professional fabrication shop.

Some large fabrication shops have fully computerized CAD/CAM capabilities. This permits a part to be designed on the computer in 3-D and then precision machined by computer-controlled lathes and milling machines. While this expensive technology might seem well beyond the scope of most small fabrication shops, that is no longer necessarily the case, at least for certain types of jobs. Recent developments in the field have now made it possible for fabricators with basic computer skills to

design parts on their PCs, have them precision manufactured, often half a world away, and delivered to their doors.

To see just how this process works, we set up an experiment based on the following: A stock car spins out on a racetrack, slams into the wall tail first, and inadvertently becomes the trigger mechanism for our fabrication test. Among the parts damaged in the crash were two rear suspension mounting brackets. The car, now undergoing a rebuild by its new owner/driver, Joe Barnes, would, as he notes, need replacements for the damaged parts.

"The rear end lower mounting brackets are also home for the coil-over shocks," Barnes says. "They are mounted to the lower part of the quick change rear end. The handling of the car is greatly dependent on the accuracy of the suspension mounting points."

Since the bracket is a custom item not available at your local parts supply store, it would have to be fabricated—in this case by Barnes and his shop assistant, Greg Scigliano.

MAKING PARTS ON YOUR OWN

Fabricating a suspension bracket job is a straightforward process, Barnes explains, involving many basic techniques that apply to your own projects.

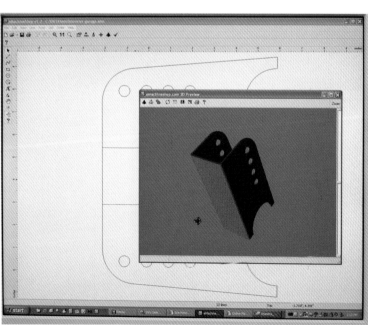

Here is a view of a downloaded race car suspension bracket, which is drawn in 3-D through an online part design program. **David Pruitt**

"First make drawings of the bracket to be replaced, and Greg and I did the job using regular shop tools and equipment," Barnes says. "We primarily used a ruler and basic mechanical drawings, then we used a drill press, saw, grinder, welder, and plasma cutter to do the rest of the work."

After making the drawing, the next step in fabricating the suspension brackets was to cut a three-inch radius section out of a 1/8x4-inch piece of flat steel using a hole saw or plasma cutter.

"We located the centerline, then sawed the hole, then cut the piece in half. Because a chop saw takes 1/8 inch out, we allowed 1/16 inch extra to allow for what the blade cuts out. The next step was to take a center punch and mark the center point for the hole saw, then drill what's called a pilot hole," Barnes adds. "We had a very defined centerline, so we drilled the pilot hole, then switched to the hole saw for the big hole."

Once the hole was finished, Barnes and Scigliano cut the piece to the proper length using two-piece sections, so that when it's split in half, all four pieces will be cut with the half circle already in place. Then they cleaned up all imperfections.

"The trick to doing a really clean job is to clamp on some kind of guide so that you have something to follow, rather than try to do it freehand," Barnes said. "This could also be done with an oxyacetylene torch if you don't have a plasma cutter. The only real difference would be in the amount of cleanup work needed."

After tacking the four brackets together, Barnes laid out the four suspension mounting points, bolting the spacers and rod ends where they would go. "In order to make sure the brackets were mounted perpendicular to the pinion gear, we used an angle finder and a level," he says.

While not part of his original bracket plans, Barnes then welded an 8-inch section of 2x2-inch, 120-square tubing on to the suspension brackets. This tubing will be used to mount the coil-over shock assembly. Some modern production cars use a somewhat similar design in that their springs and shocks are behind the rear axle.

MAKING PARTS ON YOUR PC

After a short break for some much-needed coolants, Barnes was ready to tackle the suspension bracket job

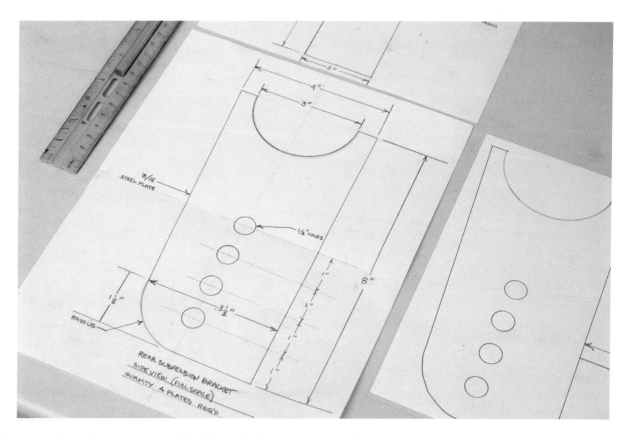

These are the plans in a more traditional fashion, as Joe Barnes drew the bracket on a 1-to-1 scale on paper before trying to fabricate it. **David Pruitt**

Here he transfers the plans to flat steel. **David Pruitt**

all over again—on his laptop. He visited the eMachineShop.com website to build a part and then compare it with the bracket he built in terms of build quality, cost, time, and so on. (There are other websites that offer similar services.)

On the website, he first downloaded the CAD drawing software to design the part. "You put it all together, using some simple commands, and then you select your material, the desired thickness, and if you're designing a complex 3-D shape, you set the height that's the third dimension of the drawing," Jim Lewis, president and founder of the business, says. "Then go to the 3-D view and actually see that your

part is what you intended it to be. The software is designed for easy use by someone with some engineering knowledge and for the total amateur who's just getting into it and doesn't know anything about manufacturing."

The downloaded software also gives warning messages about things such as certain manufacturing restrictions. For instance, if you're doing a sheet metal piece and you're bending it too close to the edge because you just want a little ridge, the software will tell you that the bend line is too close to the edge and you can't do that; instead it will recommend a distance to make the design work. Then you make a change, or-

If you're making a part the old-fashioned way, the next step after drawing out the plans is to cut the bracket's radius section with a hole saw. **David Pruitt**

BLADE ROTATION

Then make the next cut with a chop saw and grind off the suspension bracket's rough edges.
David Pruitt

Then make the next cut with a chop saw and grind off the suspension bracket's rough edges. **David Pruitt**

changes, until you get it right.

Rather than follow all of the necessary steps used to order the brackets, below are some of the main points.

With the software installed, Barnes went to the "shop menu" and selected .118-inch steel for the bracket, as this was the closest to his original specs.

He clicked on the *rectangle* button, then clicked on the starting and ending points of the rectangle, went up to the numeric bar, and entered the dimensions of 8x4 inches.

The next step was the "line menu" where he selected "machine," then selected a laser cutter to

perform the work.

Following the on-screen prompts, a 180-degree arc was drawn onto the rectangle, the four half-inch-diameter holes were put into place, as were the tapered sides, giving Barnes roughly the shape of one side of the bracket.

Back to the toolbar: he clicked on *rectangle*, selected the upper part of the design, then entered *edit-copy-edit-paste*, pulled down the control key to drop the top down to the bottom, making a mirror image to complete the bracket template in 2-D. He then entered an ungroup command to delete any extra

Next cut through the centerline to create the bracket's half circles. **David Pruitt**

Eliminate any imperfections with the grinder again. **David Pruitt**

Using a metal slug from the hole saw as a template, draw out the pattern. **David Pruitt**

Use a plasma cutter to get the correct angle. **David Pruitt**

Next mark the suspension mounting points on the four brackets. **David Pruitt**

Here Greg drills the four brackets together for exact accuracy. **David Pruitt**

This is the bracket with spacers and rod end in place prior to final welding.
David Pruitt

Barnes makes sure the brackets are perpendicular to the pinion gear. **David Pruitt**

segments (this is the computer's version of cleaning up any imperfections left after cutting a piece of steel), selected the two horizontal lines, then went to the "line machine" command and selected bend, 90-degrees.

The bracket design completed, Barnes entered the 3-D command in order to study the bracket from different angles. His request for a price for two of the brackets was answered in seconds: $128.17, including tax and shipping. The brackets would be delivered within 22 days.

When the brackets arrived at his shop, Barnes gave them two thumbs-up. "I think these and the ones I made will do exactly the same job," he says. "The accuracy is exactly the same. The website-designed ones are bent rather than three pieces welded together, which makes for a cleaner, neater job. I think what's nicer about these is that I didn't have to spend four hours of my time doing

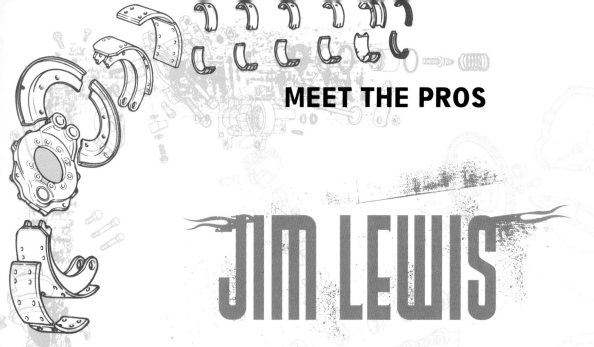

MEET THE PROS

JIM LEWIS

"If you can get the concept drawn, we can probably build it."

For Jim Lewis, who has always tinkered with things mechanical and who holds a degree in computer science, eMachineShop.com was the end result of his quest to combine two of his favorite things.

"I've been playing with mechanical things since I was a little kid," Lewis says. "I was always taking things apart and then trying to put them back together again—sometimes I succeeded. Over the years I've built up a collection of tools in my shop at home, but it was when I got my first machine tool, a hobby lathe, and saw how that dramatically increased the capabilities of what I could accomplish that I began to think about combining my machine background and the computer science background. I also had a pretty strong interest in internet business models. So I put them all together and came up with my website business."

It took more than seven years for the website to be fully operational, as the software needed to design parts took some years to create. With an official launch in 2004, the website has received orders from all around the world.

"We do a lot of parts that are transportation-oriented: automobiles, motorcycles, bicycles, airplanes," Lewis says. "We've even had orders from NASA."

Jim Lewis combined two of his loves—machining and computers—to create a successful fabrication business that makes many projects easier for the do-it-yourselfer.

MEET THE PROS

JOE BARNES

"No one was going to give me a race car, so I had to learn to build my own."

L ike Lewis, Joe Barnes has always been involved with things mechanical, but for Barnes the computer is just another tool learned out of necessity rather than a passion.

"I've always been into cars and racing," Barnes says. "My dad took me to stock car races when I was a kid. My uncle had an auto repair shop, so I sort of grew up around mechanical things. When I was about nine, I disassembled and reassembled a lawn-mower engine. I started working with my uncle when I first got my driver's license, then worked at some other shops and for a Ford dealership; until, in 1988, I bought my own shop. What really inspired me to stick with it was the fact that I love racing."

Barnes built his first race car in 1984, but didn't really get serious about it until 1989 when he built a car to race on the tracks in New England. Even though he had some success, the money and time he spent away from his family prompted him to stop racing and concentrate on his garage business. Now that his children are older and the business is flourishing, he is starting up again and is now in the process of rebuilding the car the brackets in this project were fabricated for.

Joe Barnes comparing the online-designed bracket to his hand fabricated part.

AL TEAGUE

"The more you work at it, the more you'll learn."

On August 21, 1991, a southern California hot-rodder named Al Teague did what many believed would never be done by driving a single-engine, wheel-driven car across the Bonneville Salt Flats to a two-way average speed of 409.986 miles per hour. Although it's true that others, such as Craig Breedlove,

One of the fastest men on the planet at work in his office, preparing for a record run. **Thomas "Pork Pie" Graf**

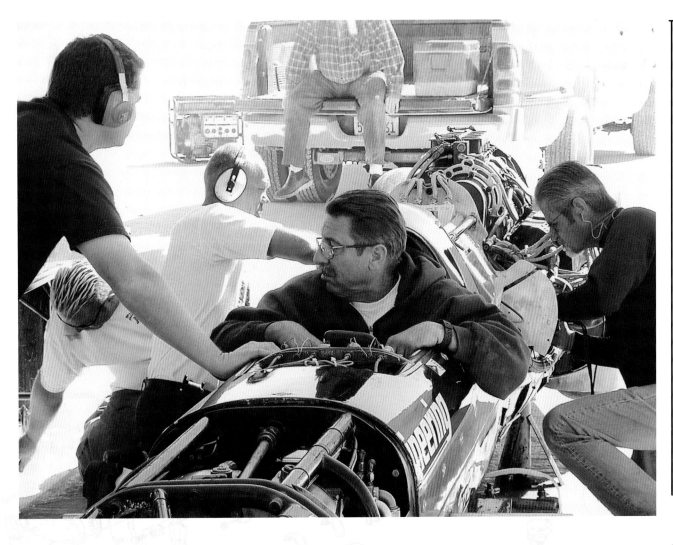

Here Al Teague performs a final systems check before he loads up for a trip to the starting line.
Thomas "Pork Pie" Graf

Art Arfons, Gary Gabelich, Don Vesco, and Andy Green, have gone faster, they did it in turbine- or jet-powered vehicles, which were more aircraft than automobile. Today, some 14 years later, Teague's record still stands.

The contrast between the current outright LSR record-breaking car, which not only broke the record, but the sound barrier as well, and Teague's *Spirit of '76* effort is equivalent to the difference between Lindberg's *Spirit of St. Louis* and the space shuttle. How was it possible for one man, working with only basic fabricating tools in a small garage behind his mother's house, to build a car without major corporate sponsorship dollars and drive it into the record books? Let's see.

"Basically the car was built with regular hand tools, a drill press, a small air compressor, an oxyacetylene welder and torch set, and an old recipro-cating saw that I bought for $40," Teague says. "The

car evolved over a number of years from its begin-nings as an open-wheel lakester with a 150-inch wheelbase. The wheelbase was next lengthened to 180 inches, and finally to the 225-inch wheelbase streamliner with the wheels enclosed that set the record. We had to move the rear wheels closer together to enclose them into the body, took the front axle and front end off, then made a new one where the wheels sit slightly offset instead of beside each other, something that had never been done before."

Although the body liner was completed in 1982, the Bonneville course had been closed due to wet weather, and it wasn't until 1984 that this car made its initial runs on the salt, turning 268 miles per hour. That was followed the next year—the last with the blown 392-ci Chrysler cast-iron hemi—with a 353-miles-per-hour run. The next powerplant, an aluminum alloy hemi race engine, provided more

The conversion from lakester to streamliner takes shape as thin strips of veneer are fastened in place, then covered with fiberglass cloth and sealant to produce the body mold. **Al Teague**

speed: 384 miles per hour in 1988, 398 miles per hour in 1989, and 400 miles per hour in 1990. The record of 409.277 set by the Summers brothers multi-engine Goldenrod in 1965 was now in Teague's sights.

Hidden under the sleek fiberglass skin of Teague's *Spirit of '76* is as fine an example of dedication and problem-solving skills as you are ever likely to come across. Fabricated entirely by hand, without benefit of wind tunnels, computer models, or major sponsorship dollars, this purpose-built car did the job it was intended to do and put its builder into the history books. Here's what went into building the 27-foot, 9-inch-long, 4,500-pound machine:

A small high-speed parachute that's used to get the car down to about 300 miles per hour. "The bottom holds the big chute, which then gets deployed to bring the car to a stop, with some help from the rear brakes," Teague says.

A transaxle out of a 1969–70 mid-engine Indy car, set up like a sprint car, with a Chevy 12-bolt ring and pinion in

it. "The entire car was built in a 20x20-foot garage. I started on the lakester version of the car New Year's Day 1975 and worked on it every day after my regular job until it was ready to go to Bonneville in August 1976," Teague adds. "Until that trip, it never left the garage."

A data equipment recorder that monitors engine functions like blower pressure, oil pressure, pan pressure, and monitors the cylinder head temps two or three times a second.

"The frame is basically just rectangular tubing put together kind of like when you built model airplanes when you were a kid and you put the sticks together and the pins—this was before the plastic ones—and we just shaped it," Teague says. "It's really strong, but it does flex some."

Even Teague would probably agree that if there is one part of the car in which inspiration outdid perspiration, it is with the placement of the front wheels.

"The FIA rules say you have to have a minimum of four wheels with two of them on a common axle; it has to be driven by a minimum of two and steered by a minimum of two, and they can't all be in one line," Teague says. "Since I didn't want a wide bulge in the front bodywork covering the wheels, like most liners had back then, I had to figure out a way to get the wheels side by side, but really close together and still have room for an axle and kingpin and all that stuff. Then I thought: What if I just moved one of them back a bit? That would open up enough room for everything. I remembered walking by a heavy equipment yard and noticing how they mounted the articulated wheels on mobile cranes and that image somehow stuck with me. Then I had to figure out how to steer it."

One night, while lying in bed, he came up with an answer: building a steering similar to a modern airplane bell crank. "I anchored it like a Ford I-beam suspension with a Dodge van steering gear shaft that turns a butterfly-type Pittman arm hooked up to a pair of drag links attached to two 1 1/2-ton truck spindles with torsion bar suspension over it and two radius rods," Teague says. "It worked, and it'll turn 20 degrees, whereas most liners only turn two or three. I can make a U-turn with it, which makes a big difference when you're going for an FIA record run because you only have one hour to get turned around and do all your maintenance for the return run, so any time saved is a big help."

Teague got into cars through his older brother, Harvey, who was mechanically inclined and started getting the first hot rod magazines back in the late 1940s. "He would buy old cars for $10, bring them home, and take them apart," Al says. "Of course, we never had the money to fix them. My dad would get them running if he could. About 1948, Dad started taking us to the motorcycle speedway races over at Lincoln Park in Los Angeles. Once I smelled the Castrol on those JAP engines, that was it.

"Everybody we hung around with back then was into cars. We started going to drag races in the mid-1950s, and about 1958 I got my own car and fixed it up—put a '56 Chevy engine in it, painted it. Harvey

and I bought a roadster together and took it to the drags every weekend. He began to lose interest, then he went into the service, and I took it over."

In the late 1960s, after spending time in the army himself, Al started going to Bonneville. In 1972, he got behind the wheel of a B/Fuel open cockpit '29 Model A highboy roadster that turned 268 miles per hour. "I raced the highboy until the lakester was ready to run in 1975," Teague says. "I ran the car as a lakester until 1981, when it set a fast time of 308 miles per hour, then started the work of turning it into a streamliner. I'm actually rebuilding the roadster again here at the shop, something to have some fun with."

As someone who had worked as a machinist and millwright, taught machine shop, engine building, and high-performance tuning classes *and* built the fastest single-engine car in the world, Al Teague knows a thing or three about what it takes to become a good fabricator.

"If you're just starting out and want to set up your own shop at home or whatever, I'd recommend you start with a good set of tools, a MIG welder, a good drill press, a small flat steel grinder, and then a little later on, a small lathe and a tap and die set," Teague says. "When you're building something, don't let little things stop you. If you don't know how to do something, chances are that someone will step in and give you a hand and pretty soon things will start coming together. Don't try to over-engineer everything— reinventing the wheel. Make it simple and chances are you'll make it work."

He also says that many people underestimate their abilities, figuring that they can't complete harder fabrication jobs. "Well, just try it and see," he says. "You might be surprised."

He's even surprised himself once in a while, like the time he went out on the salt in October 2002, and set another 400-plus FIA world record. You'll no doubt find him back at Bonneville again once the roadster is finished.

Heading for the measured mile and a drive into the record books. Both the car and its trailer are handmade with all American parts. **Leon Braskamp**

MEET THE PROS

RON KROL

"I learned from an old-school craftsman who took a huge amount of pride in doing work correctly."

Ron Krol, owner of AAA Metal Fabrication Inc. might seem at first glance to be an unlikely candidate for a *Monster Garage* episode, particularly since he manufactures stainless-steel brewing tanks and wine tanks for a living. But when you couple the fact that he is one serious biker dude and the planned build would turn a fire truck into a mobile brewery, it all fell into place.

Ron Krol is a longtime fabricator who specializes in stainless-steel containers.

Krol's journey from a metal sculpture major at the John Herron School of Art to one of the top metal fabricators in the land involved working in a variety of jobs, each of which ratcheted up his skill levels another notch, or as he puts it, "I have explored the fabricate-damn-near-anything life pretty extensively for the past 40 years."

He got his start working summers with an old pro as an apprentice pipe fitter. "He was truly an artist with molten metal," Krol says. "Just riding back and forth to work with him was, in retrospect, about a thousand times more valuable than a college education."

His advice to fabricators just getting their start is to make sure they don't overreach their talents—especially in the area of welding. "By that I mean welding a bracket or a simple plate fixture is light-years away from a titanium or chromemoly car or bike frame. Start on easy bench welding jobs and work your way up," he says. "Get a really good welder to help you. We all learned from those who preceded us. Inverter welding equipment has made welding easier and affordable to just about anyone, but it also takes getting a feel and

One of Ron Krol's creations.

understanding of the materials, and a lot of practice."

As you would expect, given the scope of the work, Krol's shop is pretty well decked out with equipment including the following:

- A 1/4x10-inch shear
- A 90-ton press break
- A 86-inch set of pyramid rolls for rolling tank cylinders
- 6 250 welders with high frequency and foot-controlled water-cooled torches
- 3 big wire feeds
- 2 plasma torches

He is currently putting in an overhead crane and a specialized spot welding machine for making heat transfer panels and is looking at getting a CNC plasma cutter.

For those looking to set up their own shop Krol offers the following advice: Make sure you have enough power, or make sure the equipment you buy fits what power you do have. A good basic setup would include the following:

- A small wire feed MIG machine
- A 14-inch abrasive chop saw
- A drill press
- A 4 1/2-inch right-angle grinder
- Vise grip finger clamps
- A steel table (great first project) about 2 to 3 feet by 4 to 6 feet with a 1/2-inch thick top with a vise mounted on a corner
- A framing square and a level

"Although I have been involved with metal fab for years, my vision for TIG welding is pretty well shot," Krol says, "so now I primarily spend my days doing 3-D CAD design work for my fabricators. I've built bikes, have a patented wine tank design, and designed and built a machine that can wash over 100 tons of potatoes per hour."

> "On the first day, Jesse made a comment about how I had the coolest hydraulics he had ever seen. That was assurance enough for me."
>
> — Todd Blandford, hydraulics expert

Hydraulics involve the science of controlling and using water pressure or the pressure of other fluids and fluid mechanics to address engineering problems. In cars, the most common use of hydraulic systems are in the brakes, where as you push the brake pedal, the pedal pushes fluid through the brake lines and against a piston, which in turn pushes on the brake pads or shoes and stops the car.

Hydraulics often involve the use of a pump to generate pressure and move the fluid, and a cylinder, which the fluid acts against and causes to move. These pumps come in many shapes and sizes. Some are capable of generating a lot of pressure with a low volume of fluid, while others use a high volume of fluid but a low pressure. Pumps will typically have two ports on them and the fluid will be pumped out of one port, while the fluid returning from the cylinder will flow back to the pump through the other. Some pumps are bi-directional, meaning they are capable of pumping fluid out of either port, while some are only capable of pumping out of one.

Pumps can operate on either DC or AC current, but Todd Blandford, the hydraulics expert who worked on the *Monster Garage* handicapped vehicle and ultimate tailgating vehicle, says he's only used DC pumps in his work. He also says that he likes to be able to adjust the pressure output of the hydraulics pump. "With the pumps I use, which are bi-directional, I'm able to adjust the pressure coming out of each port individually, meaning I can have two different pressure settings, giving me more control over my system," he says.

Cylinders, sometimes called actuators, also come in many sizes and shapes. The cylinder has two ports on it, just like the pump, one at either end of the cylinder. It also has a rod that comes out of one end. Internally, that rod is connected to a piston. "And depending on which port the fluid is coming in at, that will determine the direction of movement of the rod," Blandford says, adding that the diameter of the piston or "bore" of the cylinder is another important factor. "The larger the bore, the larger the internal piston," he says. "The larger the piston, the more surface area it has, meaning more fluid can push against it, creating more force."

Hydraulics use cylinders to lift just about anything.

On *Monster Garage*, hydraulic systems are commonly used to open doors and unfold anything from a shark cage to a wrestling ring.

The other power factor in the cylinder is its stroke, or how far the rod moves out of the cylinder. This will determine how far you can actually move something. Since the rod comes out of the cylinder, a seal must be used around the rod, so that the cylinder does not leak. This seal is what usually determines the cylinder's overall pressure rating. Pressures over the rated capabilities of the cylinder will result in leaks. One other note: You should always pay attention to the rod diameter itself. If a rod diameter that is too small is used to push against heavy loads, it could cause the rod to "bow" as it comes out of the cylinder, possibly ruining the cylinder.

Equally important is the diameter of the lines used, as well as the fitting size used. Make sure the line and fitting diameter will complement your pump fluid output. Using a pump capable of 10 gallons a minute with 1/8-inch lines and fittings would be a waste of a pump. Likewise, using 1/2-inch lines with a one-gallon-a-minute pump would be equally wasteful.

The tricky part of figuring out a hydraulics system is matching the capabilities of the pump against the capabilities of the cylinder, so that your setup moves

what you want and as fast as you want it to. The following are items you should take into consideration when setting up a hydraulics system:

The bore of the cylinder: This will determine how much force can be generated by the cylinder, and indirectly how fast a cylinder will move based on pump output.

The stroke of the cylinder, which will determine how far an object will be moved.

The fluid output of the pump, which will determine how fast a cylinder can be filled.

The pressure the pump can generate.

So, how do you figure out how all of these work together to create a well-functioning system? Here's our basic formula:

$$\text{Force} = \text{Pressure} \times \text{Area}$$

or

$$F = P \times A$$

Force is what the end result is, pressure is the operating system pressure, and area is the area of the cylinder piston. Incidentally, most cylinders are round, since a round shape is easier to seal. That said, the formula for figuring a round area is:

Area = pi x (Radius) ^{2}

If you plug that into the formula above, you get:

$$F = P \times (pi \times R^2)$$

Putting that formula to the test, let's say you want to lift something straight up that weighs 125 pounds and you have an operating pressure of 500 psi. So far, you have:

$$F = P \times A$$

$$F = 125$$
$$P = 500$$

$$125 = 500 \times A$$

$$125/500 = A$$

$$0.25 = A$$

Then remember that A equals (pi x R^2), so 0.25 = (pi x R^2)

When you divide .25 by *pi*, you get .079 or thereabouts (see below).

$$R^2 = 0.079$$

The square root of .079 is .282, making our radius a bit over 0.25 of an inch (0.282, to be precise):

$$R = 0.282$$

So, if you chose a cylinder with a bore of 0.5 inches (which means the radius is 0.25 inches), and a working pressure of 500 psi, the force would be 98.17 (see below), which is not enough to lift 125 pounds.

$$F = 500 \times pi \times (0.25)^2$$

$$F = 98.17$$

Todd Blandford, though, doesn't typically use a cylinder with a bore smaller than 0.75 inch. So if you used a bore of 0.75 inches, your force would come out to F = 220.88, which would be plenty to lift 125 pounds. With a 1-inch bore cylinder, the force would equal 392.69.

Now, let's look at how an increase the pressure instead of the cylinder bore changes the formula. Staying with a 1/2-inch bore cylinder, but increasing the operating pressure of 1,000 psi, results in a force of 196.34, which would also lift 125 pounds.

Now let's compare this another way:

Our original design called for a 0.5-inch bore cylinder with an operating pressure of 500 psi, resulting in F = 98.17

By doubling the cylinder bore to 1 inch with an operating pressure of 500 psi, the force reached 392.69.

Yet doubling the pressure to 1,000 psi with a 0.5-inch cylinder bore resulted in F = 196.34:

$$F = 1000 \times pi \times (.025 \times .025)$$

$$F = 196.34$$

As you can see, increasing the cylinder size had more of a profound effect on our system. If room for the cylinder is no problem, it's more effective to increase the bore. With the 1-inch bore cylinder, you could actually *decrease* the operating pressure and achieve the same results. A lower operating pressure is always a good thing, as you stand a better chance for a leak-free system, for a longer period of time, as well as increase lifespan of your components. If your cylinders are rated for 825 psi, it's much better to run your system at 500 psi, than 800 psi.

HYDRAULICS: WHAT ARE THEY REALLY GOOD FOR?

Hydraulics can be used in a ton of applications. If something can be moved, nine times out ten, hydraulics can move it. So the question ultimately becomes this: Is it practical to use hydraulics to move this object? It's a question only the person contemplating the project can answer. To look at ways hydraulics can be used in fabrication projects, we'll outline one that is a more common application and another that is a custom application.

BUILDING A LOG SPLITTER

One simple, yet effective use of hydraulics is in a homemade log splitter. One of Todd Blandford's friends wanted to make one a few years ago and here's how they went about it.

First, they bought a tractor cylinder from a local farm supply store, then they built the track and mounts, and plumbed the hydraulics using premade lines from a local hydraulic vendor. Blandford's friend chose a cylinder with a 4-inch bore and a 24-inch stroke. The distance between the pushing platform and the cutting edge was about 26 inches, so the pushing platform would

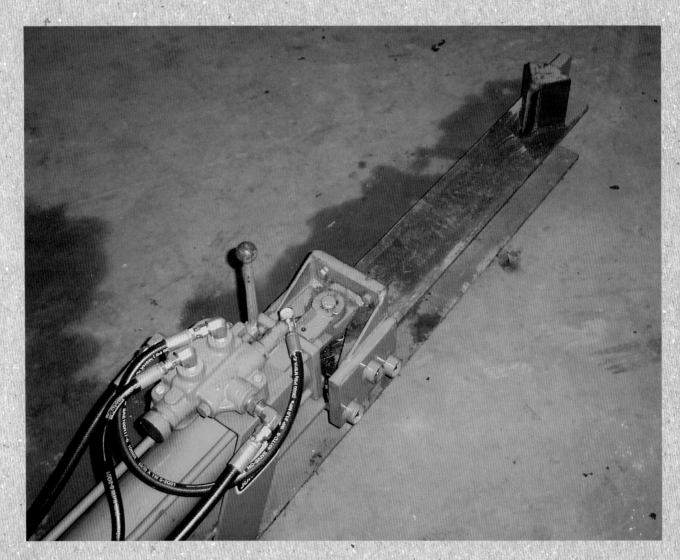

This base of the log splitter is a 6-foot length of 1/4-inch-thick H beam. The cutting edge sits at one end of the unit, while the cylinder and pushing platform are mounted at the other. The directional control valve sits atop the unit. **Ben Ganey**

This is the business end, or pushing platform. The "points" you see are nothing more than bolts screwed through the piece and sharpened. These are to hold the log while pushing. **Ben Ganey**

The cutting edge of the unit is made up of an 8-inch length of 1x5-inch flat stock, ground to an edge. Two pieces of 2x3x1/4-inch angle are turned on end and welded to the blade for support, as well as to help split the log. There is a 1/4-inch cap welded on top of the angles. **Ben Ganey**

The pushing platform is made of three pieces of 1x5-inch material, roughly 7 inches long. Gussets made from 1/4-inch material have been added for support. The platform rides on the top of the "H" beam using cam followers. One cam follower is positioned to ride on the top, while two more cam followers are positioned to ride on the bottom edge of the top surface.

never "bottom" against the cutting edge. The tractor pump generated about 2,500 psi, resulting in a whopping 31,415 pounds of force.

This project was completed rather cheaply due to the fact that Blandford's friend didn't need a pump, as he used the internal pump of his tractor. The cylinder cost about $150, which included the heavy duty clevis mounting ends. Lines ran about $120, which included tees and quick disconnects to splice off of the tractor pump lines. The cam followers cost about $60 and the steel about $20, not including the "H" beam, which was purchased at an estate sale for a cool $25. The control valve was about $75, throw in $50 for paint and miscellaneous, that brings our total to about $500. Now, go out and price one, typically they run anywhere from $800 to $1,200. Even with the cost of a pump if you don't have a tractor, this unit could be built for less than buying a new one.

This valve controls the direction of the cylinder. Pushed back, it will direct fluid to retract the
cylinder; pushed forward, it will move the cylinder rod out. It also has a neutral position, allowing
fluid to simply flow through the valve with no movement of the cylinder.

INSTALLING A HYDRAULIC DOOR ACTUATOR

The second hydraulics project involves opening and closing an automobile door. In the custom automotive field, this used to be handled by electric actuators. But these were often slow, bulky, and sometimes just plain expensive if you had some heavy work for it to do. Todd Blandford has used hydraulics on a number of car door systems and has been able to create systems that open a rear hatch in as little as two to three seconds and close it in three to four seconds. The typical electric actuator would take twice that time, sometimes three times as long.

For this project, the first step is to examine where you might want to mount the cylinder. For this example, Todd Blandford is working with opening a typical front car door. Normally, he likes to mount the cylinder under the front dash, with the rod end attached to the moving surface. This location will keep the cylinder tucked away from the passenger area.

The next step involves figuring out how long of a stroke you will need to open the door. To do this, pick a spot on the door, (Blandford usually chooses a spot near the hinge point) and mark it. Then, use a coat hanger that has been taped to the dash to measure the distance from the fully opened door to the mark on the door.

Next, it's time to make some mounts. Making the mount for the door is easier than the dash mount. Blandford often uses a simple piece of angle iron, with one hole through the top for the bolt to hold the cylinder end and multiple holes to mount the bracket to the door. If the door's sheet metal is weak, using a "backing plate" behind the sheet metal becomes necessary. This helps to distribute the force over a wider area, making the door a little stronger.

The dash mount is a harder hurdle to overcome. Blandford suggests starting with a piece of round stock that has been drilled and tapped to mount the other end of the cylinder. Next, he would weld this round stock to the largest piece of steel he could fit under the dash. "If the dash itself has no good supports, it will be necessary to cross-brace this bracket," he says. "Normally, the dash will have at least one brace that runs from the center console over to the door pillar. If this isn't very 'beefy,' plan on running at least two brackets from your cylinder mount over to the firewall."

He also notes that in a typical hydraulic door setup, you will have 200 to 300 pounds of force at these cylinder mounting points, so he recommends bolting the mounts as opposed to welding them. "If you're

The front door cylinder in place, attached between the dash and door mounts. **Freedom Motors, USA**

wrong on your placement, it's a little easier to move something if it has been bolted," he says.

Now it's time for the tricky part: figuring the exact location of your mounts. This is much easier to do with the help of a friend, Blandford says, adding, "Although I have, in a pinch, used my friend duct tape." Start by bolting your dash mount to your cylinder, and have your friend hold the cylinder in place under the dash. With the door closed, hold or tape the door mount in such a way that it lines up with the rod end of your cylinder fully closed. Then open the door, pull out the rod end of the cylinder, and check to see if it still lines up with the mount.

"A little long is OK, as it's almost impossible to get the right stroke to line up exactly," Blandford says. "If it's a little short of the mount, that means either the door will not open all the way when the cylinder is extended, or you'll need to move the mount closer to the hinge, thus using a shorter stroke to open the door. Just remember, the closer you are to the hinge point, the more force it will take to close the door. This is a leverage thing, the further out on the door you are, the less leverage it takes to close."

From here, follow these two steps:

With the door closed and the cylinder collapsed, move the hole on the door mount in or out, until it lines up with the cylinder.

With the door open and the cylinder fully extended, move the door mount in or out on the door to get the cylinder lined up with your hole.

Repeat these two steps until you have a location that works for both the open and the closed position.

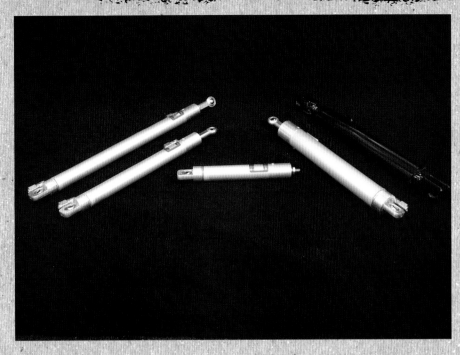

Cylinders with a variety of different bores and strokes, as well as different mounting ends. **Freedom Motors, USA**

A typical double pump-mounting bracket. **Freedom Motors, USA**

Then securely attach both mounts in place and bolt the cylinder to the mounts.

Next, you need to determine where you want to mount your pump. Blandford suggests mounting it inside the vehicle because if it is on the outside, the pump will be subject to road debris and you'll have to route the hydraulic lines *through* the vehicle floor or

Going, going, gone. This vehicle has three separate actions—gull door, ramp, and front door—all running off just one pump. It's triggered through one handheld two-button remote control.
Freedom Motors, USA

firewall. "An acceptable location would be the trunk of a car, or behind an interior panel in the case of a van or SUV," Blandford adds. "Stay away from under the hood, as excessive heat from the motor could have an effect on some materials used in the hydraulic lines."

After mounting the pump, run your lines from the pump to the cylinder. Then fill the pump with fluid, and follow the pump's instructions to bleed all the air from the system. Bleed the system with the cylinder bolted to the dash, but *not* bolted to the door, Blandford says, so that if something goes horribly wrong, it won't wrench your door from its hinges.

"This next step is really important," he adds. "I only use as much pressure as necessary to open and close the door. Since I'm able to adjust pressure in both directions, I can set the open pressure, then set the close pressure. These two values will usually be different, as it takes a bit more pressure to close a vehicle door." In fact, modern vehicles are so airtight that you can actually feel the air being pushed as the door closes, making it necessary to slightly increase

the closing pressure in an effort to overcome that air.

Blandford suggests making the pump accessible so that you can make the pump pressure adjustments easily. "I'll start with the pressure backed way off and attach the rod end of the cylinder to the door. I'll run the pump and see what happens," he says. "If the door doesn't move, I up the pressure. I'll do this in both directions, and only give it enough pressure to make it open and close securely. Once set, I will pull the pump out of the vehicle, and run it on a bench with pressure gauges attached to the pump to see what I actually ended up with. I'm checking to make sure I'm running the system within *all* component specs, so as not to over-pressurize the system."

If he has more room to push, he makes a note of the pressures required for the job, then adds 50 to 100 pounds of pressure to those figures so that the system will work in all types of situations—warm weather, cold weather, well-charged battery, weak battery. "If you built your mounts securely enough, the slight increase in pressure will have no noticeable effect on the vehicle," Blandford says. "Plus, it's a good idea to make note of your operating pressure in case you have to duplicate your work for someone else."

IS THAT ALL?

There are two more important points to remember when it comes to working with a hydraulic-operated door: First, that door we just moved with hydraulics needs somehow to be unlatched *first*, before the hydraulics can actually open it; second, we have a pump and a cylinder hooked up that we can open and close our door, but how do we actually control the pump?

First, let's tackle unlatching the door. Several companies make aftermarket door solenoids that will unlatch a door. The best place to buy one of these aftermarket parts is not at your local auto supply store—it's better to go to your local car stereo shop.

Secondly, you have to figure out how to control the pump. You can use something as simple as a switch mounted somewhere on the vehicle. But that option requires the switch to be on the outside of the vehicle, so you can actually get inside it by pushing the switch and activating the hydraulic door. A slicker approach is to use a set of remote controls to trigger some relays installed in the vehicle to run the pump.

"The pumps I use normally draw about 20 to 25 amps, while the solenoids to unlatch the doors draw about 13 to 15 amps," Blandford says. "I will use a bank of relays soldered together to form the control unit and break the unit up into an 'open' circuit and a 'close' circuit. I also always make sure the relays are capable of handling the current draw. [You need to] think about what is needed to for the 'open' circuit to work, and using simple relay logic, draw out your diagram."

He likes to break up the power supply needed by the control unit as well, use a fuse block. That way, if one thing fails on the system, not everything will necessarily fail. "Plus, it makes it easier to track down a problem if you know what fuse you are blowing all the time," he says. "I use fuses as opposed to circuit breakers because if you are having a problem and a

fuse blows, that circuit is now dead, alerting you to a possible problem. A lot of the circuit breakers will automatically reset, sometimes hiding a problem until it is too late."

As far as which remote control to use, talk to your local stereo shop guys about getting a system that is capable of outputting two *momentary* signals. One signal can be used to open everything and the other to close everything. The reason Blandford likes using momentary signals is that they are only active while you are activating the remote, thus giving you some control over how long the system runs. This can be an important safety feature, especially if you realize someone still has their fingers in the doorway as it begins to close.

WHAT KIND OF COMPONENTS SHOULD YOU USE?

Here are the parts Blandford recommends if you want to take on a hydraulics project. (Keep in mind most of his work revolves around the automotive industry; he has automated front doors, gull doors, rear hatches, and ramps on a variety of vehicles. This specilization has allowed him to narrow down what he needs to use.)

• **Pumps**: He normally uses one single pump that's capable of pressures in excess of 2,000 psi, with a flow rate of about a gallon a minute. He favors a bi-directional unit that allows him to control the pressure in both directions independently. He also likes a pump that is compact in size.

• **Cylinders**: The cylinders Blandford uses are usually a 7/8- to 1-1/8-inch bore, which give a good compromise between power and speed when used with the above pump. Some standard strokes are 6 inches for front doors, 9 inches for rear hatches, and 14 inches for doors that open past 90 degrees.

• **Control units**: Blandford makes his control units using standard DPDT relays. "This allows flexibility when designing a new system," he says. "I can control one or two pumps, up to three different door solenoids, and can even roll down one window to relieve air pressure and roll it back up again. All control is operated through a two-channel remote system."

PNEUMATICS

"With air, there's no oil all over the place." — Eric Scarlett, Episode 6 fabricator

Pneumatic operating systems work very similarly to hydraulic systems, with the essential difference being that pneumatics involve the use of compressed air rather than hydraulic fluid to move whatever it is that needs moving.

Eric Scarlett, who helped create a Porsche golf collector in *Monster Garage* Episode 6, is a seasoned expert in working with pneumatics, as he has tackled many air bag installations as owner of First Class Autowerks. He advises that even a pretty seasoned at-home fabricator leave air bag installations to an experienced professional due to the fact that the suspension system in your car or truck is critical to the safety of the vehicle.

"If it's done right, air bag suspension maintains itself, maintains its own pressure of air at all times," Scarlett says. "A lot of people make air bag kits that they claim bolts right into your car. Nothing bolts right into your car. People can say whatever they want, but when you put an air ride suspension system on your car, that is customizing your car. It's custom fitted to your car, not like the stuff that comes in a kit. For instance, take the fittings they give you; they usually have nylon quick-change ends. Put them under enough pressure and they break, they crack, they leak, they're garbage."

Another factor to consider when using pneumatics in automotive systems is that they run on compressed air, which causes condensation and eventually water and rust to metal parts. "Some people want chrome [pneumatic] tanks because they look cool, but I don't put chrome tanks in a car. I have my tanks coated on the inside to prevent rust," Scarlett says. "When rust gets into the

system, it screws up the valves and the next thing you know you're driving down the freeway and your car slowly starts dropping down and starts scraping; or you park somewhere and when you come back to the car it's lowered on one side."

"Air suspension is serious stuff," he adds. "Before you let anyone install a system in your car, talk to other people they've worked for; go into their shop and check out the quality of their work. If it's done wrong and malfunctions while you're going down the freeway at 70 miles per hour, it can kill you, and maybe some other people too. In my shop, if you can't do it right the first time, then don't do it at all."

The following photos in this section illustrate the highlights of a typical First Class Autowerks air bag installation, this one on a 1981 Chevy pickup.

Rear half of the truck with the C-notch, which allows the truck to sit lower, already installed.

The valves in place. Two valves are needed for each air bag. The installation also includes a sliver digital air-pressure sender.

The air bag mounts and spider-like cross members that hold the mounts in place. Also seen are the four-link bars that hold the axle in place.

The air compressors mounted under the engine compartment.

Front A-arms with the bag in place, lower A-arm plated, and modified upper shock mount.

The air tank mounted on the side of the frame.

The stock gas tank and axle.

The truck bed with sections cut out before the bed has been dropped and the
sections welded together.

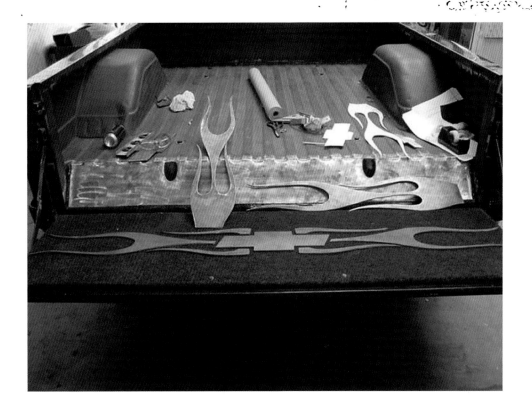

Here are the metal flames and bowtie that will be welded to the truck bed.

The truck bed after application of a bed-liner.

The completed truck lowered for its first ride.

TODD BLANDFORD

"Be leery of self-proclaimed masters."

Todd Blandford, who was responsible for the hydraulic installations on the Cadillac Escalade featured in *Monster Garage*'s "Ultimate Tailgating Vehicle," is the owner of Great Lakes Custom Creations. He has been involved in "hydros" for the past 16 years, primarily in the handicapped transportation industry.

In fact, he developed a system that uses custom-built control units with smaller-sized cylinders and pumps that react faster than the standard

Todd Blandford knows his way around hydraulics installations. That's why he was tapped to help make the ultimate tailgaiting vehicle in Episode 31 of *Monster Garage*. **Great Lakes Custom Creations**

units, which are presently commercially available. His path to this type of work began when he was a teenager in Michigan.

"My fascination with things mechanical and cars in general began at the age of 17 when I purchased my first automobile, a lime-green AMC Gremlin," Blandford says. "Shade-tree mechanics started immediately following the purchase. I replaced a front wheel bearing before I ever knew what one was, or even what its purpose was; living with the Michigan winters, bodywork followed shortly after."

After a few years spent managing restaurants, Todd Blandford applied for a job with a company that installed hydraulic systems into handicapped adapted vehicles.

"The interview went poorly, but somehow I managed to land the job anyway," he says. "Great, I thought. I have no tools, hadn't worked on a car in years, and knew absolutely nothing about hydraulics—fun times those first few months. Over the next few years, I kept my mouth shut, my eyes open, and managed to learn enough to make myself useful.

"Through trial and error, I learned what worked and what didn't, what components were best suited to what applications. I learned to weld, how to break and shear sheet metal, how to fabricate. I prototyped, refined, reworked every aspect of the system, all in an effort to provide maximum reliability for minimum complexity. I spent many long hours on the road reworking previously modified vehicles, often in bad weather, laying in driveways in the dark. But all it took was the smile on the face of the end-user to make it all worthwhile."

By 2003, Blandford had become such a hydraulics expert that he was asked to furnish the hydraulics for the *Monster Garage* Mercedes handicapped vehicle and then to take part in the Escalade build.

"On the first day, Jesse made a comment about how I had the coolest hydraulics he had ever seen. That was assurance enough for me," he says.

Blandford says the hydraulic professionals out there often use their own methods, products, and practices, so he recommends that anyone contemplating a hydraulic installation should get a second opinion about their project.

Working with plastic can help you build anything, from a wild air dam to a motorcycle windshield.

"Working with a high-tech polycarbonate [plastic] is basically like working with wood. You can use regular wood tools like a table saw; you can drill it, tap it, hit it with a sledgehammer, and you won't break it."
— Eddie Paul, Hollywood car builder

Plastics are man-made synthetics that, in certain chemical combinations, can rival the strength of the strongest steels, yet when heated can be shaped, cut, welded, formed, sanded, and painted to the point they appear to made of something else entirely—making plastics a great choice when fabricating a custom project.

Not only are the tools needed to work with most plastics essentially the same as those used in woodworking—skill saws, handsaws, sanders, drills, etc.—so are the skills required to use them. Tools that are more specifically necessary when working with plastics include hand-held heat guns, die grinders, and paint spray guns. None of these tools require anything additional in the way of shop space, lighting, ventilation, so if you have a shop set up for wookworking, you are ready for "plasticworking" too.

There is one item, however, that you should get if you really plan to do a lot of plastic fabrication. It is what Hollywood car builder Eddie Paul calls one of his most favorite tools: a vacuum forming machine. You can find plans on the internet to construct this type of machine, which can give the home fabricator the ability to make colored, textured, or clear plastics. Most of these machines can be built for less than $300.

Plastic may also be formed into various shapes using a portable shop furnace or a simple and inexpensive electric furnace operating in a range of about 250 to 400 degrees Fahrenheit.

In Paul's experience, where he's built not only cars for movie sets, but various machine-related props as well, he has worked with almost any kind of plastic out there. One such job, where he used multiple plastics and standard home tools on one prop. "The prop's parts ended up being vacuum formed over wooden plugs, rough cut with an electric chainsaw, ground down with a disc grinder, then sanded with a belt sander," he says. "Most of the wood plugs were not even all that smooth. My crew had never used plastic before so the skill level was minimal, to say the least. But the project was completed on time and, after a little paint, it looked like a showpiece; in fact it was a showpiece."

A SHARK TALE: TAKE ONE

Paul compares building a great white shark to building a nuclear-powered sub or a super computer—none of these being an easy task. But just like any job, you start with a plan or blueprint, and a list of materials. "Long ago I learned a lesson that Isaac Newton once learned from Descartes: When a problem seems too large and complicated, break it down into small problems and solve each of them individually," Paul says. "So I broke the shark down into basic problems (bite-size projects), such as, first, what will I make it out of? Well, it would be used in the ocean, so the materials would need to be made of noncorrosives such as stainless steel, plastic, brass, and/or anodized aluminum."

Next, Paul says, he considered weight. He didn't want to create an expensive anchor, so that led him to think about making the shark out of plastic materials. He decided to cast the skin out of a relatively new polycarbonate product, then add micro balloons to boost the shark's buoyancy.

The beast size, however, proved to be a tougher decision. "All the sharks we had previously tried to film were about 5 to 6 feet long," Paul says. "My assumption was that since the background of the expected shot was to be blue water, I could cheat the shot and use a smaller shark. This would save time and money, as there would be no reference for size. I decided to make the shark 18 inches long, small enough to handle but large enough to showcase some detail."

That decision wasn't in line with the client's. "When I proudly showed them my little work of art, I was a bit set back by the response. They said, 'This looks wonderful. When will ours be done?'"

Realizing that the client probably wanted something larger, Paul questioned them as to how much bigger they wanted the shark to be. "'How about 10 feet?' the client responded. "We don't want it too large!'"

TAKE TWO: BACK TO THE DRAWING BOARD

From there, Paul created a full set of templates based on a larger design and transferred them to plastic. He also tweaked the design further so that it would retain its ability to float. This included redesigning the shark's vertebrae into flat, 1-inch-wide strips of polycarbonate. These were fastened to the top and bottom of the silhouette's center spar with brackets allowing them to bow outward. "These 'ribs' were attached within a few days, and the body looked like a real shark body, minus the head," Paul says. "As soon as the head was complete, it was attached with angle brackets."

Paul says the shark's hollowed-out fiberglass head was then rough-sculpted from foam and coated with fiberglass and a layer of body putty. From there, the details on the head were carved and sanded into the body filler before a mold was cast. Then the mold was sprayed with mold release, and a fiberglass head was cast inside it.

"The new head was pulled out and set aside for painting and detail: eyes, teeth, gums, and airbrushing," Paul says. "Neither my dad nor my then-girlfriend (now-wife) Renée escaped the great white's vengeance. They were both drafted on sight into the hard labor of shaping and sanding the body and cutting the thousands of feet of polycarbonate sheet that went into making the monster. [Yet] it wasn't until we started casting the skin that life took an evil turn. When I needed it to be stiff, it was flexible; when I wanted it flexible, it was rigid. The second and third skins were better but not right. The fourth skin was the one I used."

Once the skin was complete and painted, it was installed on the skeleton and the shark

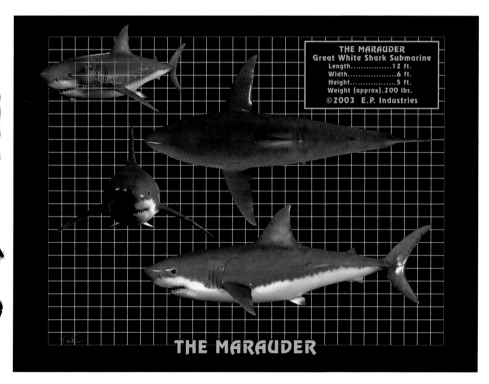

THE MARAUDER
Great White Shark Submarine
Length................12 ft.
Width...................6 ft.
Height..................5 ft.
Weight (approx).200 lbs.
©2003 E.P. Industries

THE MARAUDER

Sushi 1 nearing completion. **Eddie Paul Industries**

earned its name: Allison. Then she was shipped off.

When it finally reached its destination, as did Paul, the time came to test Allison's abilities. Paul went down in the water with her, as did Mark Blessington, a longtime deliver. "It would have been difficult to do alone because I needed to take the shark down to about 30 feet and balance her out by adding weight through the mouth," Paul says. "The weights were hung onto a cable that allowed me to pull her weight forward or rearward with a simple pulley system. The whole process took about 45 minutes, and the shark was balanced perfectly."

"The next morning, we put Allison back into the water and started filming the whites interacting with her. I had her set up so that I could operate her from a shark cage in the water. This way, I had a clear view of the area and could steer her around. Her range was limited only by the 50-foot umbilical that carried her air and allowed her motion. She looked right at home as about five or six sharks joined in to swim along with her."

To get more action for the film Paul's clients were making, they decided to make Allison look like a dying shark. "I moved a small weight onto one of the pectorals and moved the control stick in an erratic motion," Paul says. "It was as if someone had turned on a switch and run high voltage through the ocean. The sharks took on a different air, one of danger."

"It didn't take long for the first attack by the biggest of the sharks. I saw her swim directly at Allison's right-side [starboard] gill area and slowly but steadily take a large bite out of the plastic and rubber shark. She did this four more times, and within minutes my robo-shark was reduced to an expensive gutted toy. But, most important of all, we had gotten the needed shot with my reputation still intact."

For an encore, Eddie Paul decided to build a more complex great white, this one large enough in fact to carry a diver/driver inside.

TAKE THREE: A BIGGER AND BADDER SHARK

The third shark, dubbed *Sushi 1* by Eddie Paul's daughter, Ariel, ended up being a bigger and badder shark at 14 feet long and 4.6 feet tall with a diameter of 54 inches. It not only needed to look as much as possible like a real shark, but also had to be large enough for a diver/operator and be self-powered, swimming by tail motion.

The other requirements for it included the following:

- It had to have a method of entry and exit that could be operated from the inside and outside.
- It had to be neutrally buoyant with the ability to become positive or negatively buoyant when needed by the enclosed operator (pilot).
- It needed to be simple to operate and repair (in the field) and simple to load and unload in water.
- It had to be constructed from noncorrosive materials and produce no sound or electrical discharges.
- The operator would need to use a rebreather unit and must have the ability to navigate open water in a reasonable manner.
- It needed to be air powered and not expel air bubbles.
- It needed to have reasonable duration while submerged, with the pilot able to communicate with the support crew.

Sushi 1 ready for a test. **Eddie Paul Industries**

SKIN

The shark's skin needed to be flexible, strong, naturally buoyant, and easy to work with, so Paul decided to use a brush-applicable transparent urethane two-part elastomer that set up in about 10 minutes. The shark required three and a half kits of the elastomer at a total weight of 67 pounds per kit.

POWER

Paul says he chose to use pneumatic power in the shark because it could be used directly in saltwater without costly waterproof housings, and is readily available. "It can be recharged in minutes while at sea by simply changing the scuba bottle," he adds, noting that he even used a newer scuba tank that contained 140 cubic feet of air at 3,400 psi. "This opened up a more practical approach to air power; this tank is basically compressed horsepower on tap."

- The air system had to be easy to replace and there would be a video link to the outside for the ability to navigate in open water.
- Of course, all this had to be accomplished within a few months and for less than $100,000.
- The process behind the project are detailed below.

CONSTRUCTION OF THE PLUG AND MOLD

"We researched the great white, comparing photos and film of the shark from all angles, then compiled a rendered image of the shark on 3-D studio MAX for pulling off dimensions," Paul says. "This was converted to a DXF file and brought into AutoCAD for dimensional extrapolation. The 3-D image was converted into a top, side, and end view."

From that profile, he built a rotary fixture with 2-inch steel tubing that was about 48 inches wide and about 20 feet long. This tube was to be the center reinforcement tube for the shark and had bearings on each end, allowing it to be rotated. Then 2-inch-thick by 4x8-foot foam blocks were glued to this tube with foam glue spray. After that was complete, Paul rough cut the foam blocks to the silhouette of the shark by increasing the AutoCAD drawing up to full scale.

"Successive layers were then added. With each block of foam or layer of sprayed foam, we would start with chain saws and progressively convert to finer methods of sculpting until we were down to sandpaper-wrapped toothpicks," Paul says. "This process went on for about three weeks until the plug was complete and ready to be coated in preparation for the fiberglass molding process, after which it went out to a fiberglass company who shot the mold perfectly."

CONTROL

"If 'simple is better,' our controls could not be simpler," Paul notes. "A single joystick was mounted in the rear portion of the head (which tilts forward on hinges to allow entry). As the head tilted forward, the single stick control tilted forward with it. This was done for added clearance and ease of entry to the shark, feet first."

Once the pilot entered the shark body, he or she could tilt the head up (closing it) and lock it shut by toggling the controls onto the second rib back, near the front upper spine area. "This placed the control valve and control stick in front of, and slightly to the right of, the pilot," Paul says. "Then, by moving the control stick to the right, the tail moves to the right and moving it left moves the tail left. A single tail stroke moves the shark forward about 36 inches. Each successive stroke provides forward thrust of an equal amount."

TURNING

Paul's shark can be turned by the same control stick and a technique of timed movements of the stick. For instance, if you move the stick to the left for two seconds, the shark's tail will move left a full stroke. If you move the control stick to the right for one second, the tail moves right about one-half the distance. "Repeating this motion will allow the tail to act as a power device and a rudder," Paul says.

BUOYANCY

To increase buoyancy, a weight was added below the shark's center of gravity to help stabilize it and keep it oriented in the upright position. To increase the safety factor, a secondary inflatable buoyancy system [SIBS] was added. "These SIBS can be deployed [inflated] on command and will be utilized for emergency assents only," Paul says. "[The inflation of] one or two of these bags should easily bring the shark up at a reasonable rate of ascent."

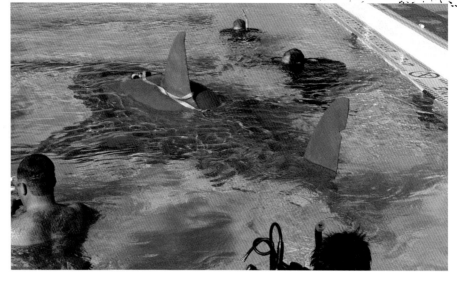

Sushi 1 was amazingly lifelike in the water. **Eddie Paul Industries**

VISION AND NAVIGATION

Navigation proved to be a bit more complicated than expected, Paul admits, because there was no sensory feedback from the outside water. "You are basically in a sealed shark with no waterflow indicating either speed or direction, meaning that the pilot had no way of perceiving speed, movement, or even direction. I would often imagine a failed swim only to come out of the shark to a jubilant crew of onlookers seeing the success of the swim," he says.

Eventually, he installed a video camera and monitor system that would give the driver a look at how the swim was going.

Needless to say, the great white did its thing, giving audiences an unprecedented look at these deadly creatures in their natural environment.

After all that work, one really has to wonder how a kid who dropped out of high school and started out working on cars and choppers in his garage end up as, well, as Eddie Paul.

"My dad was a metal fabricator; he did cars and sheet metal work," Paul says. "He taught me to weld when I was about 12. I made my first mini-bike at 12 or 13. He gave me a car to customize before I was old enough to drive."

Now more than 25 years after breaking into Hollywood, Eddie Paul is still making cars for the movies. He's worked on more than 100 films to date, and, while some things have changed, it's still basically a 24/7 operation with deadlines that would make most people crazy. For one film, his shop needed to build 220 cars in a month, and, needless to say, they got 'em done.

For those of you getting ready to set up shop to do your own metal shaping work, Paul has some words of advice. The first thing he recommends is considering your power source. "Everyone has 110 AC," he says. "If you also have a 220 AC line, so much the better, but you don't need one to get started. You're also going to need a good welder. There are a number of choices including an arc, MIG, TIG, and a number of subcategories for each of them. But if you're going to be working on normal cars made of sheet metal, you can get by with a 110 MIG machine that can be run off of a small generator or any 110 outlet.

"Most MIGs are around 100 amps and are good for 1/4-inch steel, which is fine for most automotive work. They can be bought for about $300 to $400."

The biggest mistake beginners make with a MIG is to pull the gun during the weld, when it should be pushed, Paul says, adding that only practice will help you get that down.

Another great tool he recommends getting is a plasma cutter. "They aren't cheap, but you'll find that with a bit of practice you'll be cutting metal like it was paper," he says. "If you use a piece of scrap iron or aluminum as a guide, you'll cut a line that looks like the metal was sheared off. You'll also want some of the standard manual cutting tools like shears, snips, an air hammer with cutting heads, cutting wheels, nibblers, saws, and so on."

Like our other expert fabricators, Paul's own list of tools and equipment (of which the above is only a small sample) reflects the myriad of different projects he has been involved in over the years. And, like most fabricators, you will probably find yourself buying more tools and equipment in order to do more varied jobs. Paul's final piece of advice is simple: While you're waiting for the guy with the suitcase full of money to arrive, use the time to practice, practice, practice.

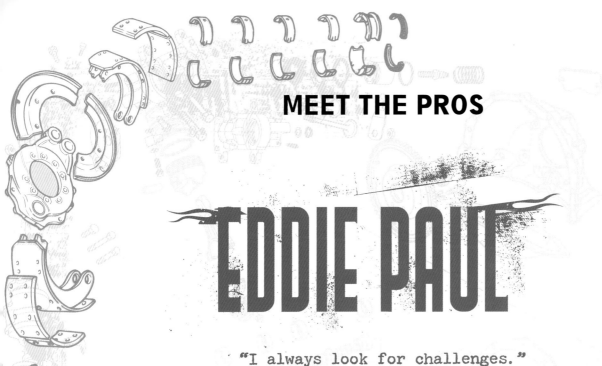

MEET THE PROS

EDDIE PAUL

"I always look for challenges."

The fact that Eddie Paul was chosen as our final master fabricator makes perfect sense as his great white shark project actually encompassed all of the previous fabrication processes featured in this book. Designing and constructing the final shark involved AutoCAD computer technology, complex sheet metal work, MIG and TIG welding, precision machining, fiberglass molds, plastic fabrication, and pneumatics.

Even though this book is about how to fabricate "damn near anything," most home fabricators reading this probably never thought that a great white shark would be included under the "anything" umbrella. Well, we couldn't let that happen, could we? In this chapter, we'll get a rare look inside the process behind constructing one of the most complex and difficult fabrication projects imaginable.

For master fabricator and inventor Eddie Paul, his life has been full of fascinating jobs. In the late 1960s, Paul started chopping motorcycles out of his garage, doing the kind of customizing, painting, and building that *Monster Garage*'s Jesse James does today.

Then when he moved into his own studio to continue his chopper building, his third customer was someone from a movie studio. "The guy said he was working on a movie called *Grease*, and the studio was in a real bind because they needed 48 cars. So, this guy says to me, 'If you can do it, this is yours."

Of course, Paul didn't have many guys working for him back in those days, so he had to go out and hire more off the street. "Then I jumped on the phone and bought all the cars

Eddie Paul has fabricated nearly anything and everything under the sun, from movie cars and custom motorcycles to mechanical sharks. **Eddie Paul Industries**

The Strata-Cycle, which Eddie Paul built in two weeks for the Rangers. It is an example of thermal-forming plastic in its highest form. "The plugs that we formed over were made from wood, and the plastics were a combination of ABS, PVC, and clear and tinted acrylics," Paul says. "The bike is now about ten years old and still looks the way it did the day we built it." **Eddie Paul Industries**

The shark being tested in the water. **Eddie Paul Industries**

A closeup look at the inner workings of the shark Paul created for movie-making magic. **Eddie Paul Industries**

I could find from the 1940s and '50s, no matter what condition they were in, put a sleeping bag next to my desk, and worked around the clock until it was done," he says. "I think we finished the last car with about five minutes to spare. From that point on there was no worry about the next month's rent."

Now the movies he's provided cars for include, *The Fast and the Furious* trilogy, *xXx,* and *Taxi.* His fabrication projects have also included re-creating antique flying machines, making miniature

submarines, constructing lightweight portable pumping equipment for fire departments and airborne laser weapon systems.

But even for Eddie Paul, who has had more than his share of difficult and unusual projects in the past, constructing a great white shark proved to be one of his greatest challenges. The shark, or sharks (as there were ultimately three), had to be able to swim in the ocean, perform on cue for a camera crew, and fool the real great whites it would be swimming with.

Three Eddie Paul prototypes. **Eddie Paul Industries**

MAKING A MAKROLON WINDSHIELD

Before delving into the construction of the ultimate great white, let's take a look at the way Eddie Paul used makrolon (a polycarbonate plastic) in a project that that has applications for a lot of home fabricators: a motorcycle windshield.

"Makrolon is great stuff to work with, a dream material," Paul says. "It's lighter than glass— doesn't corrode, doesn't rot; you put makrolon windows in your house nobody will ever break in that way. They even have some now that are scratch resistant. The safety shields in my shop are made of it."

Of course, there are things to keep in mind when you're working with makrolon. You can't weld it because it has moisture in it, which will cause bubbles to form in the plastic. "But it can be vacuum formed," he says. "You could make a whole car out of it if you wanted to."

STEP 1 One of the first steps in the windshield project is to lay out the pattern on a piece of foam core cardboard so it can be cut and placed on the vehicle for fitting. Foam core can be cut with a razor blade and is strong enough to be taped in place.

STEP 2 This section is over the headlight and fairly simple to make. Paul always starts with the center section of a design and works his way outward so the parts will stay symmetrical.

STEP 3 The rest of the parts are then measured and the outside dimensions marked down for laying out a pattern.

STEP 4 A compass is used to triangulate a point by bisecting two arcs. You may need to brush up on your basic geometry for this task, but this is the best way to find a point on a flat plane.

STEP 5 A few pieces are now in place and the windshield is already starting to take on a nice shape, even though it is composed of nothing but flat pieces.

STEP 6 With the patterns in place, the windshield will now be tested to make sure it can turn properly without hitting the frame. This is the time to trim if needed.

STEP 7 The first parts are cut from the high-tech polycarbonate and laid out to see how well they will fit with the aluminum brackets.

STEP 8 This is the point when things can get frustrating. You need to add one piece of aluminum trim at a time, drilling the holes to mount it to one piece of makrolon, then removing it to mark it for the next piece of makrolon.

STEP 9 Each time you add a new piece of makrolon, the aluminum trim has to be marked and drilled, then reinstalled for marking of the contiguous panel. You must also mark and trim the angles to match between the panels. Paul likes to leave the paper on the high-tech polycarbonate so that he can avoid having to mask it during the paint job.

STEP 10 The windshield is now in place and bolted up. This project required more than 100 bolts and 200 washers. Adding the headlight cover is the next step.

STEP 11 It requires a bit of skill to make sure all of the angles fit perfectly. The fun part of this project was painting the bike with a camouflage theme, which required a bit of airbrush work.

STEP 12 The windshield is unmasked and ready to mount. The headlight cover is then added to the front lower section. This little puppy weighed in at almost 50 pounds, but will go a long way in stopping a bullet.

STEP 13 All the parts are now coming together. Without good pattern, making this windshield could be a geometric nightmare.

STEP 14 The finished Boss Hoss *Secret Weapon* is ready to rumble with the best of them, and yes, that is a 350 Chevy in there.

STEP 15 As seen from the front, the *Secret Weapon* can stop traffic without even firing a shot from its (fake) twin guns.

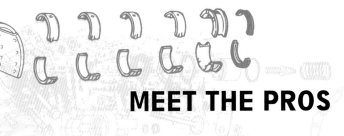

MEET THE PROS

DWAINE JUNGEN

"To be experienced, you need to experience life's lessons."

For future off-road fabrication maestro Dwaine Jungen, his career journey began, as it so often does, by following in the footsteps of others, in his case as his father's "tool-go-fer" on various projects.

For Dwaine the DARPA Challenge is yet another in a series of unexpected adventures, like the two *Monster Garage* builds, that have presented themselves over the years. Whether the Scorpion-Fox wins the two million or not, you can bet it won't be the end of the story.

As a youth, Jungen hauled junked parts home in his wagon to be, as he puts it, "dissected and scattered," then loaded into Dad's company truck and hauled off to the dump. "The turning point," he says, "was when I learned to reassemble and make the junk work. I sold quite a few 'repaired' lawnmowers."

Jungen counts his father, Bill, Uncle Tom, and select others as his mentors and teachers in things mechanical and life in general.

"All of my training has come from life lessons at the 'school of hard knocks,'" he says. "I graduated in the top of my class in high school and turned down a college scholarship because I wanted to be an engine builder. A college education is important, but it's not necessarily for everyone. College does not teach talent, ability, or desire, the way it can be learned by living."

Jungen's company, Preferred Chassis Fabrication Inc., is the owner and manufacturer of the Scorpion off-road vehicle—a remarkable machine that can cope with just about any terrain it traverses. For the past year, he has been working with the Center for Applied Research & Technology (CART) to design and construct the Scorpion-Fox, an unmanned, robotic version of the vehicle built expressly to compete in the 2005 two-million-dollar DARPA Challenge. Sponsored by the Department of Defense's Defense Advanced Research Projects Agency (DARPA), the DARPA Challenge vehicles must cover a 175-mile course through rugged desert terrain guided only by their on-board computer systems.

Here are specifications for the Scorpion-Fox that Jungen has created:
- **Chassis:** Fabricated .125-inch wall DOM tubing
- **Length:** 150 inches
- **Width:** 80 inches
- **Height:** 61 to 73 inches, variable
- **Engine:** 4BT-3.9, 4-cylinder diesel
- **Transmission:** Team RAMCO built, GM 700-R4
- **Transfer case:** Advanced adapters; 2, 4.3 gear ratio
- **Drivelines:** Tom Woods custom
- **Axles:** 4:10 gear ratio with ARB differentials
- **Wheels/Tires:** Mil spec bead lock/16/38.5x16.5
- **Shocks:** Bilstein 7100
- **Suspension:** Scorpion air
- **Brakes:** Actuated 4-wheel vented disc
- **Steering:** Dual power with electronic control
- **Throttle control:** Electronic
- **Power options:** Pure sine inverter
- **Air system:** Dual air systems
- **Control interface:** AV power products/preferred chassis fabrication (Supplies control power, sensor monitoring, and enables vehicle functions to be controlled through RS232 communication links)
- **Sensor array:** Center for Applied Research and Technology (180-degree field of view and 90-degree field of view laser measurement sensors, vehicle guidance system, global positioning system, and stereoscopic cameras
- **Navigation system:** Center for Applied Research and Technology (Four Pentium processors, cabled networking hub, and the intelligence of the autonomy control program)

For Jungen the DARPA Challenge is yet another in a series of unexpected adventures, like the two *Monster Garage* builds he participated in, that have presented themselves over the years. Whether the Scorpion-Fox wins the two million or not, you can bet it won't be the end of the story.

"Through desire, the love of what I do, and the help of many skilled people willing to share their talents, I've been able to have the success I have today," he says.

The Scorpion-Fox: Ready to rumble.

ACKNOWLEDGMENTS & PHOTO CREDITS

Acknowledgments

Los Angeles Trade Technical College
Daniel A. Castro, Ph.D., president
William D. Elarton, Construction Technologies department head

Contributing Photographers

Matthew Eberhart, Dawn McElligott, and Thomas "Pork Pie" Graf

Contact Information

Mark Carpenter: www.mtjmfg.com, www.mtjtruck.com
Jerry Bowers: www.shortcuthigh.com
Rick Dobbertin: www.dobbertinhydrocar.com
Jim Lewis: www.emachineshop.com
Eddie Paul: www.eddiepaulindustries.com
Todd Blandford: www.greatlakescustomcreations.com
Eric Scarlett: www.firstclassauto.net
Boyd Coddington: www.boydcoddington.com
Ed Federkeil: www.calcustoms.com
Ron Krol: www.aaametal.com
Al Teague: alteague@aol.com
Lisa Legohn: legohnlm@lattc.edu
Renee Newell: newellrl@lattc.edu
Joe Barnes: barnes1@ltis.net
Dwaine Jungen: www.scorpion4x4.com

INDEX

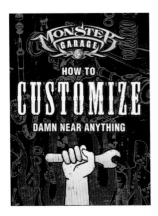

**How To Customize
Damn Near Anything**
ISBN 0-7603-1748-8

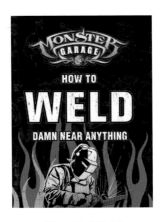

**How To Weld
Damn Near Anything**
ISBN 0-7603-1808-5

**How To Custom Paint
Damn Near Anything**
ISBN 0-7603-1809-3

**How To Build a Hot Rod with
Boyd Coddington**
ISBN 0-7603-2165-5

**How To Build a Small-Block
Chevy for the Street**
ISBN 0-7603-1096-3

**So-Cal Speed Shop's How To
Build Hot Rod Chassis**
ISBN 0-7603-0836-5

How To Paint Your Car
ISBN 0-7603-1583-3

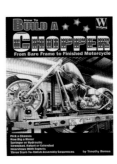

How To Build a Chopper
ISBN 1-92913-306-5